PENGUIN BOOKS

FAMILIES OF FENGSHENG

Ruth Sidel is a graduate of Wellesley College and of the Boston University School of Social Work. She has had wide experience in helping emotionally disturbed preschool children and has recently been Social Work Supervisor at the Comprehensive Child Care Project associated with the Albert Einstein College of Medicine. In the fall of 1971 Mrs. Sidel and her husband, Dr. Victor W. Sidel, visited China as guests of the Chinese Medical Association—a trip that led to her much praised book *Women and Child Care in China: A Firsthand Report,* also published by Penguin. A second trip to China, again made at the invitation of the Chinese Medical Association, has now resulted in *Families of Fengsheng.* Ruth Sidel's other books include *Serve the People: Observations on Medicine in the People's Republic of China,* coauthored with Victor W. Sidel, and a book for young people, *Revolutionary China: People, Politics, and Ping-Pong.* The Sidels live in Riverdale, New York, with their two sons, Mark and Kevin.

FAMILIES OF FENGSHENG

URBAN LIFE IN CHINA

BY RUTH SIDEL
PHOTOGRAPHS BY VICTOR W. SIDEL

PENGUIN BOOKS

Penguin Books Ltd, Harmondsworth,
Middlesex, England
Penguin Books Inc, 7110 Ambassador Road,
Baltimore, Maryland 21207, U.S.A.
Penguin Books Australia Ltd, Ringwood,
Victoria, Australia
Penguin Books Canada Limited,
41 Steelcase Road West, Markham, Ontario, Canada

First published 1974

Copyright © Ruth Sidel, 1974

Library of Congress Catalog Card Number: 74-81017

Printed in the United States of America
Typography by Martin Connell
Set in Linotype Bodoni Book and Optima

Portions of the material in Chapter 4, "Neighborhood Health Care," have
previously appeared in slightly different form in "The Health Workers of the
Fengsheng Neighborhood of Peking," by Victor W. Sidel, *The American
Journal of Orthopsychiatry*, Vol. XLIII, No. 5 (October, 1973), and in *Serve
the People: Observations on Medicine in the People's Republic of China*, by
Victor W. Sidel and Ruth Sidel, published by the Josiah Macy, Jr. Foundation.

Grateful acknowledgment is made for permission to reprint from the following
copyrighted material:
Ideology and Organization in Communist China, by Franz Schurmann.
Originally published by the University of California Press, 1966. Reprinted
by permission of The Regents of the University of California.
"Law and Penology: Systems of Reform and Correction," by Victor H. Li,
in *China's Developmental Experience*, edited by Michel Oksenberg, *Proceed-
ings of the Academy of Political Science*, Vol. XXXI, No. 1 (March, 1973).
Reprinted by permission of the Academy of Political Science.
"People's Court in China: Trial of a Divorce Case," by Doris Brin Walker,
in *The National Lawyers Guild Practitioner*, Vol. XXX, Nos. 2–3 (Spring-
Summer, 1973). Reprinted by permission of *The National Lawyers Guild
Practitioner*, P. O. Box 673, Berkeley, California 94701.

To Jerry

For introducing me long ago to political thinking and
for his continuing commitment to a better world

CONTENTS

INTRODUCTION

In THE fall of 1971 my husband, Victor W. Sidel, and I were invited by the Chinese Medical Association to visit the People's Republic of China. On that first trip we spent one month visiting the cities of Peking, Shanghai, Hangchow, and Kwangchow (Canton) and some of the surrounding rural areas. We looked primarily at the delivery of medical care, urban and rural, at the new role of Chinese women, and at the care of preschool children.

In the fall of 1972 we returned to China, this time with our two sons, again as the guests of the Chinese Medical Association, and over a five-week period in addition to revisiting the cities of Peking, Shanghai, and Kwangchow, we traveled deeper into China's interior to Shihchiachuang, Taiyuan, Yenan, Sian, and the model Tachai Production Brigade. Our primary aim in this second trip was to deepen our understanding of the organization of Chinese urban neighborhoods. We had understood from our previous visit that the Chinese urban neighborhood is a highly organized social structure that utilizes the abilities of the indigenous population to provide much of the local social, health, and welfare services. Deeply aware of the breakdown of urban life in our own society, we hoped that a clearer understanding of urban life in China might lead to a more creative examination of the causes of and solutions to the urban problems we face in the West.

Our Chinese hosts arranged for us to spend nearly two weeks visiting the Fengsheng Neighborhood in the West District of Peking, one week visiting the Ching Nian Lu Residents' Committee in Sian, and several days visiting the Kung Chiang New Village in Shanghai. In these neighborhoods we were able to talk at length with local leaders, to visit with families in their homes and to talk with them about their lives, to visit schools, factories, local health stations, and neighborhood hospitals. We were welcomed everywhere with extraordinary hospitality and warmth. Neighborhood residents and leaders painstakingly and patiently helped us to gain a clearer understanding of how they live, work, receive and deliver medical care, and educate their children.

One of the most striking characteristics of today's China is the counterpoint between the legacy of China's long, creative, and yet often "bitter" past and the startlingly new revolutionary ideology and methodology that have been at times superimposed on and at other times interwoven with the traditional. Examples of this melding of the traditional and the revolutionary can be seen in essentially all spheres of Chinese life today. In child care, for instance, the genuine belief that mothering can be shared has evolved from the extended family of former times. But now while a member of the still somewhat extended family, the grandmother, is often involved in child-rearing, mothering is also shared with representatives of the society, nursery and kindergarten teachers, who are entrusted not only with the child's intellectual development but with his emotional, physical, and political development as well. In the field of medicine there has been a major effort, more successful at some times than at others, to utilize traditional methods such as herb medicines and acupuncture along with modern Western medicine in order to preserve, in the words of Mao, the "treasurehouse of traditional Chinese medicine." The treatment of the elderly is yet another instance of the weaving together of the old and the new. Although ancestor worship and the domination of the young and middle-aged by the old had to be replaced by a new relationship between the generations, the elderly are nevertheless still respected, cared for, and considered important members of society.

It is, of course, extraordinarily difficult for an outside observer to sort out those elements that have roots in the long history of China's cities from those with newer roots in the revolutionary ideology of the past half-century. For the present leaders' greatest genius may be their perception that continuity must exist between the past, the present, and the future for the new society to function successfully, for people to feel connected to their culture and to one another. As Mao himself has said, "Let the past serve the present."

I have not attempted to present here a history of Chinese cities or a detailed analysis of those elements of today's cities that stem from the legacy of China's past. I have attempted to describe the ways people in three Chinese neighborhoods live together, using their own words in translation whenever possible. It is my hope that a deeper understanding of the exciting experiment the Chinese have undertaken will both enhance our understanding of our own society and contribute to the friendship between the Chinese and American people.

I wish to express my gratitude to our hosts in China who so graciously enabled us to make this study: to the Chinese Medical Association; to Li Chun-yen, our interpreter; to Dr. Liu Kuei, who accompanied us during our visit; to Chu Chuan-yin, the vice-chairman of the Fengsheng Neighborhood Committee; to Liu Pei-pung, director of the Fengsheng Neighborhood Hospital; to Ho Kuei-lan, leader of the Ching Nian Lu Residents' Committee in Sian; to Pan Chang-jung, vice-chairman of the Kung Chiang New Village in Shanghai; and to the countless others who generously shared their experiences with us. My thanks also to Terry Miller, who read and typed the manuscript; to Joanne Dolinar for her warm interest and editorial assistance; to Victor Sidel, who not only provided the photographs but also contributed invaluable criticism; and to Kevin and Mark Sidel, who are constant sources of insight and encouragement.

FAMILIES OF FENGSHENG

THE LIU FAMILY

"**A**ll students study for the revolution, not just for grades," declared Liu Shu-min in a quiet yet firm voice. "They usually do not think about how high their grades are but just about what their real knowledge is—for without real knowledge one cannot join the construction of the motherland!" Liu Shu-min, a lively girl of seventeen, with eyes at once smiling and serious and long dark pigtails which swing just below her shoulders, is the third oldest of the five Liu children.

Having completed six years of primary school and three years of lower middle school, she is currently in the first year of higher middle school. In her gray jacket, blue pants, green socks, and black canvas shoes she walks a few short blocks to school every morning, arriving just before 7:30. Shu-min has a long, busy day at school beginning with early-morning exercises and including classes in mathematics, chemistry, physics, English, physical culture, politics, and health. She returns home for lunch and a short rest at 12 noon, returns to school at 2:30, and then stays after classes are over at 4:00 for physical exercise until 6:00.

The wide red band Shu-min wears on her left arm indicates that she is a member of the Red Guards. When she was younger, she was picked as a "Little Red Guard," and then in 1968 at the age of thirteen Shu-min was again chosen by her classmates and approved by the leaders of the Red Guards. She and her fellow Red Guards are a far cry from the Red Guards of 1966, 1967, and 1968 who traveled long distances from home to *ch'uan-lien,* "exchange revolutionary experiences," who carried on long, intense political disputations with their teachers and with their fellow students, and who, as the vanguard of the Cultural Revolution, gathered en masse in Tien An Men Square in Peking waving and shouting, *"Mao Chuhsi wansui!"* ("Long live Chairman Mao!") as they were greeted by him. These days Shu-min and her fellow Red Guards help their classmates who may be having difficulty with their schoolwork or with their political studies; they visit historical places, museums, and parks so that they may better understand the revolution; and they help to keep order in school by preventing the five "don't wants": throwing stones, fighting, breaking school windows, playing with sticks in school, and going out of the school gate between classes.

Like the original Red Guards, Shu-min studies the writings of Mao Tse-tung and tries to use his teaching to mediate the quarrels of her fellow students. When asked to describe how she resolves quarrels between her classmates, Shu-min replied seriously, "I help them to understand the situation through their studying and applying Chairman Mao's work. We encourage them to make a 'self-criticism' and then ask them to unite." Who is chosen to be a Red Guard? According to Shu-min, "If you study Chairman Mao and your other subjects well and if you unite with your classmates well, you can be a Red Guard." According to another teen-ager who is not a Red Guard, "Red Guards have to be better than the other kids. They have to do good things and stop bad things. They have to do everything first and set an example. They have to be brave."

But it's not all studying and mediating disputes for Shu-min. Although she spends part of her free day, Sunday, washing clothes, hers and those of others in her family, she also likes to be with her friends, to go to the movies (*The Red Detachment of Women* is her favorite), and to go high jumping. She high jumps both in school and on the Peking Municipality high-jumping team. Shu-min had a ready answer and a broad smile when asked what she would like to do when she finishes higher middle school. She wants to "join the People's Liberation Army and then become a doctor." She quickly added that if this was not possible, she would do anything that was needed by her society, but after graduation her first plan is to apply to the P.L.A.

Shu-min lives with her thirteen-year-old brother, her eleven-year-old sister, and her parents in a small three-room house at the far end of a courtyard in Peking's Fengsheng Neighborhood. An older sister of twenty-four, unmarried, is a factory worker who sometimes lives with the family but usually stays in the factory dormitory. An older brother, age twenty-one, is a member of the People's Liberation Army and is stationed in South China.

To visit the Lius' one-story home, one walks down a dusty lane with high gray walls on both sides. Opposite a sign written in colored chalk that reads, "Actively carry on the sanitation movement; always keep this neighborhood clean," is the entrance to a large courtyard in which six other families also live. The smooth paths of the courtyard are surrounded by lush green bushes and trees—pomegranate plants laden with fruit, seven-foot-tall sunflowers, and small plants in wooden tubs. The bottom third of the Lius' house is gray brick, and the rest is constructed of wood painted red and green. Three small steps lead to a porch from which red pillars rise to support the slanting gray-tile roof. Just inside the front door is the main room with a stone floor and white stucco walls. A map of China and some framed pictures of the family hang on one wall over a high table on which rest a thermos bottle and glasses for tea. An electric pendulum clock set in wood hangs on another wall next to some straw baskets; a fluorescent light hangs from the ceiling, and above that a single unadorned light bulb burns. The Lius sleep in this room as well as in the other two rooms, and carefully folded quilts with red-flowered designs are stacked on the beds. By the window goldfish swim lazily in a tank set on a desk.

Shu-min's father, Liu Yen-tung, is a forty-six-year-old skilled worker in a factory in the east suburb of Peking. Dressed in a blue shirt, blue pants, and black sandals in the Indian summer of September in Peking, he is a handsome man with a broad smile and an open manner who looks younger than his forty-six years. Shu-min's mother, Chang Hung-chuang, on the other hand, looks nearly ten years older than her forty-nine years; she has a worn thin face and a worried look and is dressed in a white blouse worn over baggy blue pants. She does not work outside of the home but remains there taking care of the family. She is quiet and lets her husband do most of the talking.

Every morning Comrade Liu takes his breakfast in a small restaurant in the neighborhood and then bikes off to work at 6:30. It takes him one hour to get to work. The factory used to be located near his home, but when it was enlarged in 1959, it was moved from the West District of Peking, where the Fengsheng Neighborhood is located, to an eastern suburb. When asked if he would prefer to live closer to his place of work, Comrade Liu replied that his oldest daughter works near where they live and their children are in school here, so he would prefer to remain here and commute to work. His wife and children eat their breakfast of gruel and noodles at home, and the children then go to school—Shu-min to higher middle school, her brother to middle school, and the youngest child to primary school. They all have lunch at home with their mother, and then, after returning to school for the afternoon, the entire family eats dinner together in the evening. Just outside of the house Comrade Chang does the cooking in a tiny area which includes a coal-fed one-burner stove and a small storage space for simple cooking utensils. For dinner the Liu family enjoys many kinds of vegetables, particularly eggplant and cucumbers; they also eat some meat, chicken less often because they do not enjoy it, but fish very often because they like it.

In the evenings the children do their homework, and they all enjoy listening to the radio, playing Chinese chess, and reading the newspaper. They also very much like to go to the movies and try to go once or twice a week.

Comrade Liu works a six-day week; Friday is his day off. He spoke easily about his financial affairs. He earns 112 yuan per month (a beginning worker commonly earns approximately 35 yuan per month, and the average worker earns about 60 yuan per month), and his oldest daughter earns 33 yuan per month (1 yuan equals approximately 40¢). The implication was clear that they combine these two salaries in order to provide for the family. They pay 8 yuan per month for rent and 1 yuan per month for electricity and water. If Comrade Liu should become ill, he would go to one of the three clinics his factory maintains; for minor illness he goes to the heatlh station in his shop. If his wife is ill, she goes to the Fengsheng Neighborhood Hospital nearby, pays the entire amount, and then is reimbursed for one half of the amount from her husband's factory. The children do the same except for minor illnesses, which are cared for in school free of charge.

As the Lius and their visitors are sitting in their home talking of their medical care, a little girl about three years old with a doll-like face, wearing a brown corduroy jacket, light-colored pants, and a pink ribbon in her hair, wanders in and climbs up on the bed. Li Hsiao-hung lives in the same courtyard and is so comfortable in the Liu home that she seems like one of their children. She sits swinging her legs from the high bed, soberly looking around, and when a visitor brazenly picks her up to give her a hug and to practice meager Chinese, her eyes only widen farther. She wanders into other bedrooms with the Lius, their guests, and representatives of the neighborhood committee, all of whom seem to know one another intimately. Each bedroom has two beds piled with folded quilts, a large chest, and a small chest of drawers with a mirror hanging on the wall nearby and, next to it, a picture of Mao Tse-tung. Outside of the Liu home are large tubs of goldfish; the Lius say that they belong to a neighbor next door who does not have any children.

The lanes and courtyards of the Fengsheng Neighborhood are quiet on a weekday morning. Children are in school, most of their parents at work, leaving only a few older women, retired workers, and small children around the courtyards. Just before noon children stream out of the nearby schools and start home for lunch, some walking two-by-two, some running and shouting, others talking in small groups, the red scarves of the Little Red Guards and the red armbands of the older Red Guards standing out vividly in the crowds. Midafternoon is once again quiet, sleepy, but starting at four o'clock, children and adults begin streaming home, bicycle riders stirring up the dust of the narrow lanes, ringing their bells insistently to warn pedestrians out of the way. The streets become jammed with shoppers buying food. But by midevening dinner is over, and by nine or ten the courtyards are quiet once again.

The Liu family and six other families live together in their courtyard; these seven families are part of the fourteen thousand families who make up the Fengsheng Neighborhood in Peking. Perhaps we can glimpse some of their goals and their realities, the ways in which they and families in other neighborhoods in urban China live and work, and the ways in which their current patterns of organization relate to their past.

CHAPTER 1

CITIES IN TRANSITION: From Liberation Through the Cultural Revolution

> The Chinese city remains today what it has
> been for a century, an area of concentrated
> human residence. Residence, not production,
> remains the foundation of city life.
> —Franz Schurmann, *Ideology and
> Organization in Communist China*

THE HISTORY of China's cities stretches back nearly four thousand years. For centuries imperial authority established walled cities as administrative centers in otherwise rural areas. Many of today's important metropolitan and industrial centers such as Shanghai, Kwangchow, Tientsin, Taiyuan, and Loyang were old *hsien*, or county, capitals and have survived dynasty after dynasty, thus preserving a continuity from ancient times until today. China's cities expanded and their number grew over the millennia until in the thirteenth century Marco Polo could report: "For I tell you there is no doubt that in the vast province of Manzi [South China] are altogether quite 1200 cities, besides castles and towns of which there is a great quantity, all fair and rich."[1]

Urban dwellers in traditional China were ruled indirectly through urban organizations, guilds, occupational groups, family clubs, and clans. Rural-based people had migrated into the cities under the auspices of occupational associations and settled into neighborhoods in occupational groups; city officials could therefore maintain contact with the migrants through these associations and through indigenous neighborhood leaders.

When the Kuomintang assumed power in the 1920's, it essentially took over the existing forms of urban organization and extended city government further downward by dividing the cities into districts. Below the district level the only subdivisions were the police stations, which were established in various sections of the city and were responsible for supervising the people in that area. In the summer of 1940 the Japanese occupiers introduced the *paochia* system, which had a long history in rural China, into Tientsin and later into other cities in occupied China. According to Franz Schurmann, "Each group of ten households was organized into a *p'ai*; each ten *p'ai* formed a *chia*; each ten *chia* formed a *pao*. . . . Each unit had a designated leader who became the link between the local police authority and the population."[2] The *paochia* was clearly thought of as an extension of the local police department and was used by the Japanese and later the Kuomintang solely to control the population.

Cities faced severe disorganization during the civil war that followed Japanese occupation. When the Communists occupied the urban areas in 1949, they found chaos—inflation was rampant, food was in short supply, and human services had broken down. Ezra Vogel writes of the situation in Kwangchow:

> When the Communist troups entered Canton, they found the city in turmoil. The main Kuomintang forces had departed hastily toward Hainan Island and high Kuomintang officials and businessmen had flown to Szechwan or Hong Kong. Some underlings remained in hiding to assess the possibility of staying on. Some of the lower elements of society, taking advantage of the hasty departure of "bourgeois opportunists," were looting deserted homes and the stores and gathering goods abandoned in the streets. Some remnants of the Kuomintang army and the civil defense forces continued minor sabotage and sniping, and the targets were the Communist cadres who

walked the streets with their eight-cornered hats or their green uniforms. Inflation was rampant, the city was filled with transients, and both armies had sorely taxed the local food supply.[3]

During the first decade after Liberation, the assumption of power by the Chinese Communists in 1949, the Chinese government faced severe problems in its attempt to govern the cities. These included the need to cope with ever-increasing rural to urban migration, to deliver human services to large numbers of people, to develop successful methods of social control over the urban population, to stem the anomie that seems to be endemic to modern industrial cities, and to involve people politically in their own governing. The Chinese were well aware that a lack of participation in determining the events and institutions of one's life can lead to a sense of alienation, dependency, and subsequent resentment and anger. Although the Chinese government has used bureaucratization extensively in dealing with the myriad of problems it has faced, it also attempted to develop mass participation and indeed has tried to balance and blend the two.

The Communists had developed their techniques for organizing communities and mobilizing the population during their years in Yenan (1935–1946) following the completion of the Long March. They had special problems in Shensi province, as the villages were small and the peasants lived near the edge of starvation. They therefore needed creative economic measures to ensure survival and creative political methods of governing to bring about some form of socialism. Many of the methods and beliefs have remained with the Chinese to this time and are evident in an examination of the current rural and urban policies.

During 1942 the leaders decided to launch a campaign for rural cooperativization. An editorial that appeared on January 25, 1943, in the newspaper *Chiehfang Jihpao* under the title "Let's Organize the Labor Force" explains part of the philosophy behind the cooperativization efforts during the Yenan days:

> Those who have labor give labor; those who have animals give animals. Those who have much give much; those who have little give little; human and animal power are put together. Thus, one can avoid violating the seasons and is able to plow in time, sow in time, and harvest in time.[4]

But mutual aid was crucial not only as an economic technique but also as an organizational and educational tool in remolding the thinking of the Shensi peasant. The editorial continues:

> Because everyone works together life is active, morale is high, and there is mutual stimulation, mutual competition, and no one wants to be behind the others. The driving pace of work is just as the masses say: "Work for Work, Everyone Exerts Himself to the Bone."[5]

It was during these days that the Communist leadership began to see the importance of developing and using indigenous leadership in governing the towns and the rural areas. Since kinship groups had been pivotal in the organization of traditional China, the Communists began recruiting indigenous leaders from the peasantry, from among the kinship groups, and brought them into mass organizations and eventually into the Communist party.

In order to understand further the legacy of the Yenan period, it is necessary to consider the concept of *tzu-li keng-sheng*, usually translated as "self-reliance" but more accurately translated as "regeneration through one's own efforts." *Tzu-li keng-sheng* has been a factor in Mao Tse-tung's philosophy since the 1930's when the Chinese were attempting to turn back the Japanese invaders. As early as December 27, 1935, Mao stated: "We Chinese have the spirit to fight the enemy to the last drop of our blood, the determination to recover our lost territory by our own efforts [*tzu-li keng-sheng*], and the ability to stand on our own feet in the family of nations."[6] The essential meaning of *tzu-li keng-sheng* is that the Chinese must themselves transform China, must "stand up" in order to join the community of nations.

The concepts of *tzu-li keng-sheng* and *yi kao tzu-chi li-liang* ("relying upon one's own strength") became the key to Communist domestic policy during the Yenan days when the Communists labored under the dual burdens of the enormous poverty of Shensi province and the Japanese blockade. Illustrative of these principles on the domestic front is the tale of a model brigade, led by Wang Chen, which was sent during this period to a "wretchedly poor wasteland" where they were given title to land on which they were expected to farm, to build industry, and to raise animals. Wang Chen's vivid description illustrates the concepts of self-reliance and self-help that have become known as the Yenan Way:

> When I led my troops here to start our first army-production project four years ago, there were no caves or houses for us to live in, there was no food to buy, there were no tools, and no farmers whom we could ask to work for us.
>
> The Border Region as a whole was so poor at that time that we could not bring enough food and scarcely any implements. We received little money from the government in Yenan. Right from the beginning we had to provide for ourselves almost everything we needed. We cut down wood for primitive shelters and dug a few caves. We reclaimed a bit of land each to get some vegetables. We didn't have enough to eat in the meantime.
>
> To have something to exchange for the goods we needed most urgently we cut hard pines, which the people in the adjoining areas liked for coffins, and sold them to the villagers. The magistrates in the area through which you rode helped us

borrow some old tools from the peasants who were ready to assist as much as they could. Our tool problem was solved at last when one of my soldiers, Wang Company Commander Liu, discovered a big, old iron bell on the top of a hill in a long abandoned temple. It was too heavy to bring down and I don't know how it ever got up there. Liu dug a big hole underneath and smelted it on the spot, and we found some blacksmiths who were willing to teach our men how to make tools from the 2000 pounds of iron we got from the bell and from scrap we collected in the distant villages.[7]

Thus the principles of *tzu-li keng-sheng*, of mutual aid, of encouraging popular participation in government, and of the development of indigenous leadership have remained key in the Communist governing of urban as well as rural areas since the Yenan days.

The Communists were finally able to establish order in the cities with the assistance both of the local police and of the military. They abolished the *paochia* system; until the establishment of residents' committees in 1951 no urban administration existed below the district level. Instead local police stations began to take on civil responsibilities, and ad hoc mass organizations led by local party members or activists were formed to meet specific needs in health or sanitation. These efforts, however, were fragmentary, since leadership in any one neighborhood was not unified.

In 1951 the first residents' committees were established in Tientsin and Shanghai, the same cities in which the Japanese-sponsored *paochia* had been most successful. One of the earliest was established in Hsueht'ang Street, Tientsin, in October, 1951. According to Schurmann,

Hsueht'ang was a working-class quarter, consisting of 114 households or 531 persons. Most were workers in state-owned factories. Sometime in 1951, the city government dispatched an "experimental work team for administrative construction" into the neighborhood to organize the residents. The 114 households were divided into fifteen residents groups. These groups, after suitable education, elected 19 residents representatives of which 16 were housewives. In October 1951 a delegates meeting was held, and the urban residents committee was formally established.[8]

In addition to the central task of mediating disputes, the representatives of the new residents' committees organized literacy classes and sanitation work and dealt with some welfare problems. In 1952 residents' committees and neighborhood committees were established in Tientsin; both were set up in residential districts only and were basically a device for organizing the unorganized, the unemployed women, and the elderly.

The tasks of the new residents' committees were (1) to serve as a transmitter of government policies from higher urban authority to the people; (2) to perform public security functions and organize fire prevention, sanitation work, welfare work, mediation, and cultural and recreational activities; and (3) to serve as an intermediary for the transmission of ideas and requests from the people to the government level. (It is startling how closely descriptions of the tasks of residents' committees today resemble the description of tasks outlined in 1952.) The residents' committee was directly responsible to the neighborhood committee, which in turn was the administrative level the city administration used to relate to the people.

There was clearly some relationship between the old *paochia* system and the new residents' committee functions, particularly in the areas of public security. The residents' committees, however, moved far beyond the old public security functions of the *paochia* in attempting to meet the needs of the population and to mobilize them in determining the patterns of their own lives.

Eventually the residents' committees moved into such areas as food rationing and the granting of certificates to people who wished to leave China. They therefore became the local branch of urban government closest to the people and were run by members of the masses themselves. From the start, women played an important role in the workings of the residents' committee, often gaining power at that level when they had little at higher levels.

The residents' committee system was not extended to all cities until 1954, when a series of governmental directives was issued. The standing committee of the National People's Congress on December 31, 1954, approved three directives that set out the administrative framework of police stations, neighborhood committees, and residents' committees.

Neighborhood committees would be established as branches of the city government in all the major cities of China. They were mandatory in cities with over 100,000 population, optional in cities between 50,000 and 100,000 population, and not expected in cities of fewer than 50,000 population. Interestingly, the jurisdiction of neighborhood committees was exactly the same as that of the police stations. Officials of the neighborhood committees were selected by the district city government and not by the residents.[9] There were reports that the neighborhood committees and residents' committees were unpopular with the people, as they were seen to some extent as an invasion of family privacy and as an extension of the local police system.

By 1957 rural to urban migration had increased significantly, and consequently large numbers of unemployed dependents of urban workers had crowded into the cities. Statistics indicate that the urban population rose at a rate of 7 percent a year from 1949 to 1957, compared to a mean annual rural increase of 1.4 percent. The urban population rose from 58,000,000 in 1949 to over 99,000,000 in 1957.[10] To meet the needs of this new urban population, the Chinese government tentatively and experimentally established new kinds of urban organization. This was the time of the Great Leap Forward, of the establishment of urban and rural communes; it was a time of ample harvests, of enthusiasm, and of hope that an integrated way of life—one that would combine work and leisure, physical and intellectual endeavors—might be at hand.

A variety of blueprints were used to guide the formation of the urban communes. Some were organized around existing factories and encompassed not only the employees of the factory but their neighborhood dwellings as well. The hope originally was that factories in suburban areas could be joined together with agricultural areas to form a large commune in which workers, peasants, and students could live together and work together. This goal was never realized.

The second type of commune was based around government organizations or schools with production or work departments added to provide employment for family members of the staff of the institutions. A third type was organized around residential areas in which workshops were established to bring production into the residential areas. Still a fourth kind of commune organized in small cities might be called the heterogeneous type. In this format large state-owned factories were brought under the administrative aegis of the urban commune, thereby combining collectively owned workshops and state-owned factories under the same administration. This was a rather unusual arrangement, as state-owned factories were generally kept separate from smaller collectively owned workshops. However, this form of organization more closely resembled that of the rural communes, in which the commune structure has power over the state-owned unit.

Although the Chinese Communist dream of creating an integrated and collective living and working community in the cities of China was to last for only a brief time during the late 1950's, nowhere was this dream better represented than in the Chengchow Textile Factory Urban People's Commune. The Chengchow Urban Commune was located in the province of Honan in the heart of the great North China Plain. Chengchow, the capital of the province and its largest city, had a population of 766,000 in 1957. Its industry was light and oriented to agriculture, the primary activity of the province.

While the factory was the center of the urban commune, all of the people in the surrounding residential area, over ten thousand of them, were drawn into the commune as well. It was, therefore, an example of the first type of urban commune described above. The commune combined work and a residential environment, politics, education, and military service. The commune administered two agricultural production brigades, one sheep-milk station, dining halls, nursing rooms, nurseries, and kindergartens. Schools of all kinds, including night schools, were established. A university with nine departments—foreign languages, technology, Marxism-Leninism, industry, finance and economics, agriculture, medicine, cultural education, and military exercises—was developed utilizing work-study principles. Every unit of the commune was organized along military lines: Neighborhoods were organized militarily, and young people between the ages of sixteen and twenty-five were given military instruction. Demonstrating the power of the factory within the commune, Schurmann reports that "the factory director became the commune chairman. The factory Party committee became the commune Party committee. The factory deputy director in charge of management became the full-time deputy chairman of the commune."[11]

One of the overall goals for the commune was to become as self-sufficient as possible. To further this goal, satellite workshops were set up around the larger factories to work for the larger factories and, in addition, to produce consumer goods and services for the commune members. Ten satellite factories were established; backyard steel furnaces, smelting shops, and toy factories were developed as well. All units within the commune came under commune control, including adjacent farm areas and the peasants who worked on them. Workers in the factories went into the fields to do agricultural work, and the fifteen hundred unemployed dependents of workers were put to work within the commune's factories and satellite factories.

The hope was that more of life would be lived collectively, and with household duties minimized and work provided for all, that this would be a time of equality for men and women. By 1960 fifty-eight public dining halls staffed by 175 cooks had been established in the Chengchow commune. Some of the Chengchow restaurants grew their own vegetables; the cooks worked in shifts around the clock, and when necessary, they delivered food to the homes of the sick and the elderly. However, in spite of the fact that the cost was kept low, the dining halls were felt to be uneconomical, so much so that Chou En-lai in 1959 at the Second National People's Congress commented specifically on their inefficient use of grain.[12] Efforts were made to correct the deficiencies of the dining halls, but by 1961 their use had diminished considerably.

Other neighborhood services were established to ease the burden of household tasks on working women. Service stations frequently staffed by the elderly helped with the washing and mending of clothes, the cleaning of the house, shopping, baby-sitting, and running errands. Crèches, nurseries, and kinder-gartens were established.

But problems existed as well. Some units of the Chengchow commune were state-owned—that is, under the administration of the Honan provincial government. The textile factory was state-owned, the satellite factories were state-owned, and the agricultural production brigades were state-owned. But other units such as banks, post offices, and stores were "collectively owned"—that is, under commune control. There were wage differentials and welfare benefit differentials between those who worked in state-owned units and those who worked in collec-tively owned units. Those who worked in the latter earned a lower wage and were entitled to fewer benefits than those who worked in the former. Medical care, for example, then as now was free to workers in state-owned factories, their dependents paying half of the regular fee, and workers in collectively owned units had to pay half the cost.

Between 1958 and 1960 the Chengchow Textile Factory Urban People's Commune grew enormously. By March of 1960 it consisted of five branch communes, each of which was organized around a state-owned enterprise. Approximately 25,000 employees and workers, nearly 14,000 dependents of employees and workers, over 1,000 personnel of service industries, and over 1,500 peasants belonged to the commune. It was characteristic of the Great Leap Forward that the communes were labor intensive rather than technology or capital intensive and that they were organized to utilize large segments of the population that had previously not been working.

During this period administration in other cities was reorganized to utilize the structure of the urban commune. Contradictions existed, however, in their structures with regard to administration, production, and living. As an administrative unit the urban commune was part of a city-wide administration system, as a production unit it was part of a state-owned enterprise, and as a living unit it was meant to be an entity unto itself. These functions began to conflict, and these conflicts plus the intensive drive on the part of cadres (administrative officials, often though not always members of the Communist party) toward production, toward collectivization of family life, toward work, and away from consumerism and recreation produced strains within the urban commune. Ultimately the urban commune movement was to fail in China. The ideal of an integrated way of life based around the work situation and under one administrative aegis was essentially discontinued. However, street industries, which were largely developed during this period, have persisted to this day. Although some minor private enterprise seems to have existed in the early to middle 1960's in China, since the Cultural Revolution all urban enterprise has been brought under either state control or control of the neighborhood committees.

Although China's urban neighborhoods today may seem to us in the West to be far more integrated than anything that we know, they are organized around the residential areas rather than around production. As Schurmann states, "The Chinese city remains today what it has been for a century, an area of concentrated human residence. Residence, not production, remains the foundation of city life."[13] Thus at the end of the commune experiment the Chinese government was still left with the problems that it faced in 1958: the problem of creating economic capabilities to match the rising urban population and the problem of creating a sense of community that would reduce the feelings of anomie and alienation so characteristic of cities in both the West and the East. The urban commune movement did not solve either one of these problems, and during the Cultural Revolution in the mid and late 1960's the Chinese continued to grapple with these issues.

The Cultural Revolution was a time of massive political upheaval, of profound evaluation of both methodology and goals, and of a power struggle between the forces of Mao and the forces of Liu Shao-chi, the titular head of state since 1959. Liu and his allies on the Central Committee ran the superstructure, controlled the party cadres and bureaucrats, the party schools, and the labor unions, all in the name of Mao Tse-tung. But while using Mao's mystique and name, they tended, in the words of Edgar Snow, to slight "Mao Thought in performance. They tended to put economics before man, encourage effort by material incentives first and zeal second, push production without class struggle, boost technology by relying on 'experts,' put economics in command of politics to serve technology, and favor the city over the countryside."[14]

During the sometimes bitter struggle that followed the putting up of the first "big character poster" (a newspaper written in large characters usually put up on a wall and generally used to criticize a policy or way of thinking) at Peking University, Mao's aim, again according to Snow, was "to proletarianize Party thinking and, beyond that, to push the proletariat really to take power for themselves, and in the process to create a new culture free of domination by the feudal and bourgeois heritage."[15] From the middle of 1966 until mid-1969, the super-structure of China's government was severely cut back; about 80 percent of Peking's cadres were sent to May 7 schools (named after a 1968 directive of Mao's), where they were to reeducate themselves about socialism through the study of Mao Tse-tung Thought, discussion, and physical labor; schools and universities were closed, and along with many of China's other institutions, they underwent a period of "struggle, criticism, and transformation." When these institutions reopened, it was often under the leadership of revolutionary committees com-posed of the "three-in-one combination" of representatives of the mass (those people who worked in the institution), members of the People's Liberation Army, and workers from local Mao Tse-tung propaganda teams (later replaced by rehabilitated cadres). These last two components of the revolutionary com-mittees were frequently necessary to rescue the institutions from the chaos into which some of them had been catapulted.[16]

The urban neighborhoods also suffered from excesses during the Cultural Revolution on the part of Red Guards, students from the local schools, who rampaged through courtyards searching out and destroying the Four Olds (old ideas, old cul-ture, old customs, and old habits). According to one Red Guard:

> Usually we began at one end of a street and worked our way to the other end. Using the police records as guides, we hung signs on the gates of every house that held a Black element. . . . We

would then go back and search each house individually for old things. . . . In practice, we confiscated things like vases and furniture decorated in the traditional way. If they had revolutionary decorations, like pictures of Mao Tse-tung or PLA men, we left them alone. Statues and religious articles were either confiscated or smashed.[17]

With the onset of the Cultural Revolution residents began to protest what they felt to be abuses on the part of the local neighborhood cadres. It was felt that cadres had become an entrenched group that had subtle advantages over the rest of the population and that they had lost their contact with the people. It was also felt that cadres along with other Communist party members and professionals were becoming a new elite.

One of the primary goals within the urban neighborhoods during the Cultural Revolution was to democratize the leadership and assure greater participation on the part of the masses. During the period of the development of the urban communes leaders of the residents' committees had been elected by the people, but members of the neighborhood committees were most often appointed by the district-level authorities. Even at the residents' committee level the candidates were often suggested by party members, and in this way cadres and party members exercised informal control. The consolidation of this informal control by the local elite during the urban commune movement was severely criticized during the Cultural Revolution. Residents also protested the scarcity of employment in the local neighborhoods and the massive mobilization of students to work in the countryside and in the border areas. The target population for the rustification movement, which was originally launched in 1957, was the educated youths who had not yet been assigned jobs in the cities, young people who were neither attending school nor working steadily, and cadres whose skills were not needed in the cities but were needed in the countryside.[18] Although it was hoped that young people and cadres would volunteer to resettle in the rural areas, according to one observer, "an appeal to the youth's altruism is often backed by thinly concealed pressure and threat."[19] It is little wonder that urban youths would be reluctant to leave the comparatively comfortable, familiar urban life surrounded by family and friends for the uncertain, far more primitive, and perhaps hostile life in the hinterland. Nevertheless, 292,000 secondary-school graduates were resettled in the countryside between early 1962 and early 1964, during 1964 more than 400,000 primary- and secondary-school graduates were resettled, and in the first eight months of 1965, 250,000 more graduates were sent out of the cities.[20] This urban-rural migration was to cease at this time because of the onset of the Cultural Revolution and was not to recommence until 1968.

The process of restructuring the urban neighborhoods often involved street debates in which, according to Janet Salaff, "Residents would release pent-up grievances against the existing power structure [the neighborhood cadres], inspiring others to join in and support a power change."[21] (This is strongly reminiscent of the Speak Bitterness meetings of the 1930's and 1940's, a technique the Chinese used to arouse anger in the general population and then to mobilize the people to take a greater role in determining their own destiny.) After the cadres had engaged in self-criticism and admitted their errors, they were then free to join the masses and the other liberated cadres.

Shanghai's first revolutionary committee was established in Ku-ling Road in the densely populated Whangpoo District in May, 1967. The twenty-two-member committee, representing a constituency of 11,000 families with 46,000 people, was composed of sixteen representatives of various local mass organizations, three representatives of the district organizations of government workers, and three representatives of local revolutionary organizations; sixteen were women, and sixteen were

party members. During the early period of selecting revolutionary committees, debates and wall posters discussing the merits
and deficiencies of the candidates were very much part of the
process; however, even when residents were in a position to
participate alongside cadres, they still felt grossly inadequate.
To encourage greater responsiveness to the needs of their con-
stituents, members of the revolutionary committees were encouraged to go door-to-door to listen to the opinions and views
of the people.

Simultaneously political study was encouraged in the urban
neighborhoods. There is some indication that groups were first
organized along geographic lines and had limited success. After
a period of time some groups were reorganized along social
lines, so that women would gather together in one group, children in another. In some areas study sessions were attended by
entire family units, and family study within the home became
popular. In this sort of meeting family members could confront
one another, and the more militant youth and students could
influence the less militant older people.

In certain of the neighborhood meetings Mao's writings were
read and discussed in combination with a recollection of the
residents' sufferings in the "bitter past." The readings included
Mao's sayings and specific directives, "The Three Constantly
Read Articles" ("Serve the People," "The Foolish Old Man
Who Removed the Mountains," and "In Memory of Norman
Bethune"), and were used during the early part of the Cultural
Revolution to encourage the people to rebel. Mao's directive of
May, 1967, discussed

> the importance of overthrowing the power holders in the
> neighborhood; how to distinguish the people in authority tak-
> ing the capitalist roads; encouragement for the street dwellers
> themselves to carry out revolution without relying on the
> cadres, Red Guards, or workers; the need to reform the public

security substation; and the importance of continuing struggle against the five-bad elements [people who have committed crimes, rightists, people who belong to "bad classes"—former landlords, businessmen, and rich peasants—those with relatives living overseas, and people suspected of being hostile toward the government].[22]

Local neighborhood criticism sessions encountered problems, of course: Some residents were reluctant to criticize people in authority, and others used the criticism sessions to discharge specific grudges against specific cadres or other residents. In the summer of 1968 neighborhood study sessions were taken over by members of the People's Liberation Army, by worker propaganda teams, and by retired workers in an attempt to over-come factionalism and to connect the study sessions to other revolutionary activities in the neighborhood. As part of the effort to overcome the animosity that had sprung up between differing factions and to consolidate the work of the Cultural Revolution, "heart-to-heart talks" were encouraged, and mem-bers of propaganda teams often worked with each faction sepa-rately and then attempted to bring them together.

Political study has continued and still plays an important role in the neighborhood. Usually each major political directive is studied in the residents' study goups. (It was said that the decision to invite President Richard Nixon to China in 1972 was discussed in every study group throughout China and that many dissenting voices were heard.)

As the conflicts of the Cultural Revolution subsided, the Chinese were once again experimenting with methods of involv-ing people in governing themselves and with providing full em-ployment and basic services through a use of the concepts of self-reliance and mutual aid. Chinese institutions as well as small groups and individuals within the society seem to progress in a cyclical fashion from a period of experimentation to a period of criticism and self-criticism, followed by retrenchment and then a repetition of the cycle. Thus the methods used by the neighborhoods described in this book will in all likelihood come under severe criticism by the Chinese themselves at some future time and will be somewhat revamped or modified, and new and experimental measures will be introduced to aid urban dwellers to live together more effectively. By the time an observer thinks he understands a facet of Chinese society, it has, by then, almost surely changed, for the Chinese are committed to constant evaluation, to vigilance against the entrenchment of any elite, and to seeing the revolution as an ongoing process.

NOTES

[1] Marco Polo, quoted in Glenn T. Trewartha, "Chinese Cities: Origins and Functions," *Annals of the Association of American Geographers*, Vol. XLII, No. 1 (March, 1952), pp. 69–93.

[2] Franz Schurmann, *Ideology and Organization in Communist China* (Berkeley, Calif.: University of California Press, 1966), p. 369.

[3] Ezra Vogel, *Canton under Communism* (New York: Harper and Row, 1969), p. 46.

[4] Quoted in Schurmann, p. 420.

[5] *Ibid.*, p. 421.

[6] Mao Tse-tung, *Selected Works*, Vol. I (Peking: Foreign Languages Press, 1967), p. 170.

[7] Wang Chen, quoted in Mark Selden, *The Yenan Way in Revolutionary China* (Cambridge, Mass.: Harvard University Press, 1971), p. 252.

[8] Schurmann, pp. 374–375.

[9] *Ibid.*, p. 378.

[10] Theodore Shabad, *China's Changing Map* (New York: Praeger Publishers, 1972), p. 35.

[11] Schurmann, p. 388.

[12] Janet Weitzner Salaff, "The Urban Communes and Anti-City Experiment in Communist China," *China Quarterly*, Vol. XXIX (January, 1967), pp. 82–109.

[13] Schurmann, p. 399.

[14] Edgar Snow, *The Long Revolution* (New York: Random House, 1971), p. 16.

[15] *Ibid.*, p. 15.

[16] For a spellbinding account of the Cultural Revolution in one institution, see William Hinton, *Hundred Day War: The Cultural Revolution at Tsinghua University* (New York: Monthly Review Press, 1972).

[17] Quoted in Gordon A. Bennett and Ronald N. Montaperto, *Red Guard: The Political Biography of Dai Hsiao-ai* (Garden City, N.Y.: Anchor Books, 1972), p. 75.

[18] Pi-chao Chen, "Overurbanization, Rustification of Urban-Educated Youths, and Politics of Rural Transformation," *Comparative Politics*, April, 1972, pp. 361–386.

[19] *Ibid.*, p. 367.

[20] *Ibid.*, pp. 367–368.

[21] Janet Weitzner Salaff, "Urban Residential Communities in the Wake of the Cultural Revolution," in John Wilson Lewis, ed., *The City in Communist China* (Stanford, Calif.: Stanford University Press, 1971), p. 300.

[22] *Ibid.*, p. 305.

CHANG CHANG-PIAO

"**B**efore Liberation life was very hard. Our life was worse than an animal's. Very often we did not have enough to eat, and even when we were paid, we couldn't get any rice because salaries were so low and the price of food was so high. My wife and daughter lived in the countryside where my wife worked for a landlord. She rented land from the landlord, planted grain and vegetables, and had to pay him sixty percent of what she grew; she could keep only the remaining forty percent. We had no medical care; sometimes we were not sure if we even had life." Chang Chang-piao, an elderly retired worker with prominent cheekbones in his lean face, his gray hair receding, sat on the bed in his small Shanghai apartment and told about his "bitter past."

"Before we moved here in nineteen fifty-three, we had only one very old table, two stools, and a three-wheeled used bicycle." Now Comrade Chang's older daughter, a lively, smiling young woman lessly clean two-room apartment in Shanghai's Kung Chiang New Village. Blue, white, and yellow flowered curtains hang at the windows; the larger room is crowded with a bureau, a table, several chairs, and a large bed piled high with brightly colored quilts and pillows covered with white ruffled cases. A Mao poem describing the civil war and land reform during the 1930's and reproduced in Mao's own calligraphy hangs above the bed.

Comrade Chang's older daughter, a lively, smiling young woman with tousled hair, is a twenty-nine-year-old factory worker in Kiangsi province, south of Shanghai. She had returned home to be married to a young man who is currently working in a factory in Harbin in China's northeast. They were both given a month's holiday, after which they will return to their respective jobs. Eventually they hope to be together and work in the same area. Comrade Chang's younger daughter is a shy twenty-four-year-old worker in a local chemical factory.

Chang Chang-piao spoke of Shanghai before and after Liberation. He spoke in Shanghai dialect which his new son-in-law translated into Peking dialect so that the Peking-born interpreter could translate into English. "Before Liberation," according to Comrade Chang, "the best parts of Shanghai were occupied by foreigners; the Chinese people could only live in the poorer places. Before nineteen forty-nine the working people had no power, but after nineteen forty-nine, when the foreigners left, we working people became masters of our own destiny. We were happy to see the imperialists leave," Comrade Chang declared quietly but firmly, "and we have improved our life, but it is just a beginning; we must try to improve it more."

CHAPTER 2

SETTING THE SCENE: Peking, Sian, Shanghai

> Gone . . . the pompous wealth beside naked
> starvation.
> —Edgar Snow, *Red China Today*

The old residents still remember the Communists' entry into
Peking on January 31, 1949. The enemy had withdrawn several
days before and the town, its electricity supply cut off, was
living in a state of expectation. One evening, the lights suddenly went on, and the Liberation Army, headed by its band,
made its entry, in a general atmosphere of gaiety. On October
1st the same year, Chairman Mao Tse-tung proclaimed the
foundation of the Chinese People's Republic and hoisted the
red flag of New China in Tien An Men Square.[1]

PEKING, the capital of China during ancient times, has again
assumed political preeminence. Peking's importance, established at the beginning of the historic age because of its geographic position, has alternately increased and diminished over
the centuries. Its greatest period was almost certainly during the
late thirteenth century when Kublai Khan moved his capital
from Karakorum to the grand new city that he built and named
Khanbalik (Peking). The early Mings transferred the capital
to Nanking briefly in the late fourteenth century, but in 1421
Peking, which means "northern capital," resumed political
leadership. The city was changed significantly by the Ming
rulers, especially Yong le, the third Ming emperor, who rebuilt
the Imperial Palace during the first quarter of the fifteenth century. It stands today essentially unchanged. In 1928 the Na-
tionalists transferred the seat of government back to Nanking,

but in 1949, with the assumption of power by the Communists, Peking was once again named the capital.

Today Peking is divided into nine districts, five city districts and four rural districts. Workers bicycling to work form a steady stream particularly in the mornings and early evenings up and down Chang An Chieh, the wide thoroughfare that runs east-west past Tien An Men (Gate of Heavenly Peace) Square. They peddle slowly, ringing their bells incessantly to warn others of their approach. The center of the huge street is empty except for cars, all of which are government vehicles and taxicabs, as there is no private ownership of automobiles.

If one follows Chang An Chieh farther to the west and a few blocks north, one arrives at the Fengsheng Neighborhood in the West City district. The Fengsheng Neighborhood covers 1.5 square kilometers and contains two main streets and 132 lanes. A lane, or *hutung*, is a small street often with high gray walls on both sides; every few yards a door opens into a courtyard full of trees, plants, and flowers. It is here that the people live. The roofs of the walls and the houses are gray tile, and the sides of the streets are covered by a beige sandlike dust. But inside a courtyard the scene comes alive with color.

The main shopping streets in the Fengsheng Neighborhood are busy at all times of day: A woman is selling vegetables on a sidewalk, carefully weighing each person's purchase; a restaurant is ready for the next rush hour with a bunch of chopsticks standing in a glass in the center of cleanly wiped tables; a supermarket selling everything from candy and cigarettes to fruit, vegetables, soft drinks, fish, meat, and cookies is crowded with shoppers in midafternoon. A clothing store carries ready-made clothes and fabrics—flowered blouses for women for 3 yuan, 58 fen (approximately $1.50), men's shirts for 3 yuan, 85 fen (almost $1.60), a child's shirt with a zipper up the front for 3 yuan, 5 fen (approximately $1.25), a toothbrush for 50 fen (20¢), sneakers, toys, flashlights, a colorful thermos, and intri-

cately woven baskets. A shop to buy rice is next to a shop that
sells only various kinds of tea. As the afternoon wears on, school-
children appear carrying their khaki green bags over one
shoulder, some of which have *Wei Renmin Fuwu* (Serve the
People) embroidered on the front, adults squat waiting for a
bus, and women with formerly bound feet hobble along as if on
small stilts. Much business is carried on outside on the side-
walks: A man is selling brooms, a glazier is cutting a piece of
glass to size while his customer waits, a shoe repair man has his
place of business at the corner where the sidewalk and a tiny
alley meet, and a group of men crowd around watching two
others playing Chinese chess on a step.

Toward five o'clock the lanes become busy and crowded with
returning children and workers. All around, the dust is raised
by people returning home on their bicycles, and the old women
who remain at home come to the doorway of the courtyard to
watch the others returning to the neighborhood.

Chu Chuan-yin, a man with a serious diamond-shaped face
who appears to be in his early forties, is the vice-chairman of
the Fengsheng Neighborhood Committee. "The neighborhood
committee is the basic or lowest organization of government
power in the city," he explained to visitors as they sat around
a long conference table covered with a white tablecloth and tall
covered teacups in a large airy room in the Fengsheng Neighborhood Hospital. Two of the walls of the room are entirely com-
posed of windows; a large picture of Mao Tse-tung hangs on
one of the two remaining walls; at the other end of the room
hangs a poem of Mao's reproduced in his own calligraphy.

According to Comrade Chu, 14,136 families live in the
Fengsheng Neighborhood, a total population of 52,978 people.
Of that population 22,808 are working people, in both factories
and offices. Of the other adults 7,762 are retired workers, housewives, and retired cadres. There are four nurseries and kindergartens to care for some of the 6,146 preschool children in the

neighborhood, and there are 16,262 primary-school, middle-school, and college students.

Comrade Chu continued: "The neighborhood committee is responsible for administering six neighborhood factories, which employ fifteen hundred workers, the nurseries and kindergartens, and one service department including eight service stations such as a watch repair shop, a clothing repair shop, and a shop to repair electrical appliances. We also administer the neighborhood hospital, the house management department, which is responsible for the repair and distribution of houses in this area, and one production group, a home industry for housewives who wish to work in their homes. In addition our neighborhood is divided into twenty-five residents' committees, which range in size from four hundred families in the smallest residents' committees to eight hundred families in the largest."

The Fengsheng Neighborhood has a leading body of twenty-seven members, elected in March, 1968, during the Cultural Revolution. Seven members are full-time cadres, administrators who are often but not always members of the Communist party; the other twenty are part-time members of the committee. There has been an attempt to balance the committee somewhat according to age and sex—the elderly, the middle-aged, and the young are represented, and sixteen members are women. Ten of the twenty-seven members are government cadres selected by the district level and sent to the Fengsheng Neighborhood to work. These government cadres may or may not live in this area; the chairman of the Fengsheng committee, Hsu Chung-chi, does not live in the neighborhood, but the vice-chairman, Comrade Chu, does. In addition to the ten government cadres on the committee there are two members from the People's Liberation Army and fifteen representatives of the "mass" who have been selected by the units in which they live or work. Comrade Chu described the selection process: "The teachers in the primary school, for example, get together and elect two representatives to be on the neighborhood committee. The teachers select their representatives by thinking through their own views on neighborhood matters first and then evaluating whether the representatives will represent them correctly. They also must consider the work of the representative in her own unit. Representatives are first chosen by their units and then approved by 'higher authority.' "

The Fengsheng Neighborhood Hospital has one representative on the Neighborhood Committee, the director, Liu Pei-pung, and the service department has one representative. One housewife is chosen for every two or three residents' committees. Thus the neighborhood is governed by representatives sent down from district-level committees and by representatives indirectly elected by the people living in the neighborhood but approved by committees at the district level and by the party. It is, of course, extremely difficult to assess the relative strength of these two groups on the neighborhood committees, but this is indeed an example in microcosm of the democratic centralism under which China itself is run.

Sian

One of China's ancient cities, Sian, lies in the fertile plain of the Wei River in Shensi province, one of the two provinces (the other is the neighboring province of Shansi) that make up the region known as the loesslands of China's northwest. The area is covered with a layer of yellow silt whose thickness ranges from an average of five hundred feet to as much as a thousand feet; the silt, or loess, was carried by the wind, it is thought, from the Ordos Desert of Inner Mongolia. The Wei River valley, the economic and population center of Shensi, produces millet, kaoliang, barley, wheat, and oats on its terraced hillsides. Cotton, tobacco, melons, and grapes are grown as well.

Industry has been significantly developed since 1949—cotton mills, factories that manufacture agricultural machinery and mining equipment, and an electronics and electrical-engineering industry.

The provincial capital and possibly the most important center in the northwest, Sian has grown significantly from a population of 787,000 in the 1953 census to an estimated population of 2,400,000 in 1972. Today Sian is a busy metropolis, symmetrical in design, with two main streets dividing the town and meeting at the center where the bell tower, the center of the Imperial City during the Tang dynasty, still stands. Both the old Ming drum tower and the bell tower have been faithfully restored, as have so many of the ancient Chinese buildings and temples. Near the north gate within both the Ming and the Tang cities in the west-central district of Sian is the Lian Hu district. Lian Hu, one of the five districts into which Sian has been divided, was itself divided into ten urban communes in 1958 during the Great Leap Forward. Sian's urban communes are comparable to neighborhoods in other cities but retain the older designations, which most other cities have discarded.

Forty thousand people, 9,100 families, live in the Ching Nian (Youth) urban commune and are governed by a nineteen-member revolutionary committee. According to Wang Hsiu-chen, a full-time commune staff member in her mid-thirties with a strong, serious angular face and a quiet, competent manner, "The commune administers forty-three factories, five primary schools, one hospital still under construction, and twenty-six residents' committees. Twenty-five cadres, sixteen men and nine women, are employed by the commune to manage the commune's affairs. These cadres are divided into three groups: a political group in charge of study and propaganda work; a production group in charge of the work in the factories; and an administrative office, which is in charge of everything else."

Comrade Wang felt that the work of the political group and the production group was quite "simple" but that the work of the administrative office was rather more complicated.

One thousand twenty-two people, 302 families, live in one of the twenty-six residents' committees in the east section of Ching Nian Lu (Youth Road) and hereafter will be simply referred to as Ching Nian Lu. The three blocks in which they live are constructed similarly to the Fengsheng Neighborhood in Peking—high gray walls on both sides of the street with entrances every so often leading to courtyards. The people of Ching Nian Lu, from the commune cadres to the small children, were warm and welcoming to their strange foreign visitors; we felt a genuine sadness when we left them.

Shanghai

Shanghai, the largest city in China and on the continent of Asia, one of the largest cities of the world, has a population of ten million. Although located in Kiangsu province, Shanghai is an independent city responsible directly to the central government. Pre-Liberation Shanghai perhaps epitomized the contrast between the life of the foreigners in China and those relatively few affluent Chinese on the one hand and the great masses of poverty-stricken Chinese on the other. Perhaps Edgar Snow has provided the most vivid description of both the old and the new Shanghai:

> Gone the glitter and glamour; the pompous wealth beside naked starvation; gone the strange excitement of a polyglot and many-sided city; gone the island of Western capitalism flourishing in the vast slum that was Shanghai.
>
> Good-bye to all that: the well-dressed Chinese in their chauffeured cars behind bullet-proof glass; the gangsters, the shakedowns, the kidnappers; the exclusive foreign clubs, the men

in white dinner jackets, their women beautifully gowned . . .
the opium dens and gambling halls; . . . the beggars on every
downtown block and the scabby infants urinating or defecat-
ing on the curb while mendicant mothers absently scratched for
lice; . . . the jungle free-for-all struggle for gold or survival
and the day's toll of unwanted infants and suicides floating in
the canals.[2]

Today's Shanghai is clean, busy, teeming with people. Barges
and sampans crowd the Whangpoo as strollers by the river take
pictures of one another. The tall buildings built by the foreigners now house the Bank of China or the Revolutionary Committee of Shanghai. Heavy industry increased significantly
during the 1950's and 1960's, particularly in the production of
iron and steel, machinery, chemicals, and automobiles. However, in spite of this shift to heavy industry, Shanghai is still
China's largest textile producer.

The Yang Pu district is located in the industrial northeast
section of the city; the bulk of its 900,000 residents work in
textiles and machine manufacturing. Within the Yang Pu district
64,000 people, 13,000 families, live in the Kung Chiang New
Village, which was built between 1952 and 1956.

According to Pan Chang-jung, the vice-chairman of the
neighborhood revolutionary committee, a small, dark-skinned,
compact man who talks in an organized, no-nonsense manner,
"Before Liberation, this was a small village, the village of Yang
Chia Pang. Two hundred families lived here; there was only
one primary school. Today we have ten primary schools and
seven middle schools serving twenty-seven thousand school-
children; we have seven nurseries and four kindergartens caring for two thousand preschool children."

The families of Kung Chiang live in three- or five-story stucco
apartment buildings. Clothes hang out of the windows, and the

streets are planted with small young trees, which are seen throughout China. The village is surrounded by factories five to twenty minutes away by bicycle, in which 90 percent of the Kung Chiang residents work. When one of the neighborhood residents was asked why the apartments are not built higher, she replied that it would not be convenient for the many older people who live there if the buildings were too tall, as there are no elevators.

The Kung Chiang Neighborhood Committee is made up of thirty-three members. Again according to Comrade Pan, "The masses in each residents' committee recommend certain people to be members of the neighborhood committee. They then choose one representative to deliver the names. The representatives from each residents' committee meet together, discuss the entire list, which was gathered from among all the residents' committees, and pick thirty-three out of the list of names. This list must be approved by a 'higher-level committee,' that is, the district revolutionary committee. When the final list is drawn up, the representative will bring it back to the residents' committee and will report any discussion which took place regarding the nominees. The masses will then discuss the names again and might even recommend other names. However, the final list picked by the representatives is usually approved by the residents' committees. All final names which make up the neighborhood committee must have originated from the people; if the name was not recommended by the masses, it cannot be on the final list of neighborhood committee members."

The present neighborhood committee of Kung Chiang was chosen in 1968 in direct response to the Cultural Revolution; before the Cultural Revolution the neighborhood committee was selected entirely at the district level. According to Comrade Pan, there are no further elections planned at the present time. The eleven delegates do make an effort to select a somewhat representative group on the committee; they choose from among the old and the young, among men and women, and women, in fact, constitute 60 percent of the committee.

NOTES

[1] Nagel's Encyclopedia-Guide, *China* (Geneva: Nagel Publishers, 1968), p. 410.

[2] Edgar Snow, *Red China Today* (New York: Vintage Books, 1971), pp. 503–504.

CHAO HUAN-CHING

Chao Huan-ching, chairman of the Wu Ting Residents' Committee and head of the Wu Ting Health Station, is sixty-nine years old. His receding hair is black, sprinkled lightly with white. Wearing a white shirt, blue pants, and black canvas shoes, he greets visitors warmly and talks of his life and his work in a relaxed manner. His comfortable two-room home is just across the courtyard from the lane health station, separated by tall plants with large green heart-shaped leaves, huge sunflowers, and a large ceramic pot in which goldfish swim. Comrade Chao lives with his wife and his grandson, a twenty-three-year-old factory worker, in a brick and wood house with a tile roof. Their two rooms are separated by a wall of carved wooden designs, and in the larger room Comrade Chao sits on one of the two comfortable chairs covered with purple corduroy. His bed is piled high with bright quilts, and a desk sits in one corner. One of Mao's poems, a picture of Mao, and some of his quotations decorate the walls. A small brown radio is on top of the chests in the corner of the room, and cactus plants decorate the window ledge outside of the house.

Comrade Chao describes his life: "Before Liberation I worked as an apprentice but lost many jobs, as there often was no work and life was poor. I joined the Eighth Route Army in nineteen thirty-eight and fought in central Hupei province. I knew of Pai Chu En [the name the Chinese gave to Norman Bethune, a Canadian physician who treated the soldiers of the Eighth Route Army during the same period] but did not know him personally.

"I did not come to Peking until after the Liberation. Then I lived in another neighborhood and worked as a cadre until nineteen sixty-five when I retired. Since then we have been living in the next lane in a different residents' committee, but in nineteen-seventy when the people of Wu Ting Residents' Committee needed a new chairman, they asked me to move here."

Comrade Chao and his wife have five children; two live in Peking, and three have moved to Kweichow province to work.

In discussing his responsibilities as chairman of the residents' committee, Comrade Chao emphasized the areas where his role in the residents' committee overlaps with his role as head of the health station: "If, for example, both parents are working and one of their children becomes ill, I would make sure that the child received medical care. I often help these families, as we are all neighbors, and I am very familiar with all of them."

CHAPTER 3

THE RESIDENTS' COMMITTEES

> If a person truly loves his neighbor or truly
> is his brother's keeper, then he has a moral
> and social duty to correct his brother's short-
> comings. If truly no man is an island and
> the actions of each person directly affect the
> lives of all others, then the "group," how-
> ever defined, has a real and direct stake in
> controlling the actions of its members.
>
> —Victor H. Li,
> "Law and Penology: Systems of
> Reform and Correction"

FOUR HUNDRED and sixty-six families live in the two dusty lanes
bordered by high gray walls, half brick, half stone, that constitute the Min Kang (People's Health) Residents' Committee
in the Fengsheng Neighborhood. Of the total population of
1,658, the residents' committee is actively responsible for only
the 265 older housewives, the 118 men over the age of sixty,
the 513 students, and the 18 women of working age who remain
at home as housewives. Working men and women are under
the aegis of their groups in their places of work.

The head of the Min Kang Residents' Committee is Chang
Sheng-eh, a plump forty-three-year-old mother of four, whose
short dark hair is pulled back behind her ears and whose loose-
fitting white shirt is buttoned up to the neck on a warm Indian-
summer September afternoon. Comrade Chang has lived in
Min Kang for ten years and was elected to her present position
in April, 1971, after having been a group leader for one year.

Her husband is a factory worker; her oldest child, twenty-one years old, is at the university; her nineteen-year-old is a factory worker; her third, seventeen, is a kindergarten teacher; and her youngest child is in middle school. Comrade Chang and her family live within the same courtyard at right angles to the Min Kang Health Station. Her traditional two-room house is decorated along the front with carved wood, and the two spacious rooms are separated by a wall of intricately carved dark wood which works its way around thick, parchmentlike paper.

The position of head of Min Kang became open when the former head moved to another residents' committee. At that time the retired workers, cadres, and housewives met in one of the courtyards to discuss the situation with a cadre from the neighborhood committee who led the meeting. Usually all the people who are eligible to vote come; only the very old or the ill stay away. After the neighborhood committee cadre explained the situation, the residents then discussed likely candidates for the position of head of the residents' committee.

According to the vice-head, Chang Hsin-kuan, the residents try to choose "those who will serve the people wholeheartedly. The people know who worked very hard as group leaders." First, many names are suggested, and because more people are always nominated than are needed to fill the jobs, the attempt is made to narrow down the list. Then everyone votes, not by secret ballot, but by a show of hands. The person who receives the most votes becomes the head. Another vote is taken for the vice-head. Neither the head nor the vice-head receives any pay or does any other work, except perhaps for work in the production group.

Chang Hsin-kuan, the forty-five-year-old vice-head, is the mother of five children who range in age from twenty-three to ten. Her husband is a worker in a musical-instrument factory in East Peking. Comrade Chang and her family have lived in this neighborhood for ten years, and prior to being elected vice-head, she had been a group leader for three or four years.

Group leaders are chosen through a similar selection process as the head and vice-head. In Min Kang there are about fifty families in each group, and each group has a leader and vice-chairman, all of whom are usually housewives. Both the group leaders and the head of the residents' committee are responsible for organizing study sessions, for organizing sanitation work, and for settling disputes.

Comrade Chang Hsin-kuan gave examples of the disputes that they must mediate: "In March, nineteen seventy-two, children from two different families were very friendly, and after school they would play together. Later they quarreled, and then their families began quarreling. They came to us to settle their dispute, and we advised them to unite. We also sometimes solve marital disputes; these disputes occur mainly because of children or because of elderly parents. We urge the couples to unite also. The chairman, the group leader, the husband, and the wife will talk together, and if necessary some neighbors might also attend. Sometimes the whole family attends, the young people and the elderly included. First, the chairman talks, and then the others tell what has happened. But we have very few marital disputes, as most people grasp the revolution and promote production and have no time for this sort of thing," Comrade Chang declared matter-of-factly.

In attempting to understand relationships between family members and the techniques used to mediate disputes, it must be stressed that the individual in China sees himself quite differently in relation to his environment than does the individual in the West. While the Chinese are clearly concerned about their personal lives, they see themselves at the same time as part of a larger scene—as part of the society, as part of the revolution—and consequently, one's obligation is not merely to achieve a "happy" or "fulfilled" life for oneself but also to participate actively in the larger world. Thus in this context couples can be urged "to unite and grasp the revolution." And a judge in a divorce case can tell a husband who has admitted to "feudal ideology" toward his wife and has admitted to beating her: "You are hereby formally reprimanded by this court. We charge you to do your utmost to correct your behavior and erroneous attitudes and we charge you to see that you carry out in your actions what you have promised here in open court this morning. You are a doctor. As a doctor in a socialist state you have a great responsibility. Try in future to conduct yourself so that you can lead a happy family life with your wife and two children, and this will also help your country and comrades."[1] Thus personal happiness is not the ultimate goal or even expectation but rather a subtle interplay between personal well-being and the role or contribution one can make to one's environment.

Comrade Chao Huan-ching, head of the Wu Ting Residents' Committee and of its health station, organizes the 180 housewives and retired workers of Wu Ting into study groups in addition to his other responsibilities. These groups meet on Mondays, Wednesdays, and Fridays, some from 8:00 A.M. to 10:00 A.M. and some from 2:30 to 4:30 in the afternoon. Liu Ju-chin, vice-chairman of the Brick Tower Lane Residents' Committee, also part of the Fengsheng Neighborhood, describes their study sessions:

> On the mornings when our study groups get together, the members start coming after breakfast carrying their little stools. There are white-haired retired people, mothers carrying babies and grandmothers pushing tots in carriages. They sit in a circle, laughing and chatting, until the group leader declares the class in session. . . .
>
> Our studies are along the lines of the general program followed throughout the country by groups like ours. We read and discuss articles from the newspapers or *Red Flag* maga-

zine, or works by Marx, Engels, Lenin, Stalin and Chairman
Mao. The guide explains difficult points. Sometimes the period
is used for transmitting Party and government policies and
directives or to organize activities in our lane.[2]

Comrade Liu describes how the residents try to apply what
they learn in their study groups to everyday life. In addition to
caring for their grandchildren's physical needs, grandmothers,
because of their involvement in study groups, gain greater
awareness of the importance of teaching their grandchildren to
"love their studies, love labor, have concern for the collective
and fight against bad people and bad actions."[3] Mediation
efforts are also encouraged:

> One day after study, Chi Yen-yun of group 4 thought "Chair-
> man Mao urges unity but the two families in our yard aren't
> getting along just because of a quarrel between their children.
> They have no conflict of basic interests, why can't their differ-
> ences be solved?" When she brought the question up with the
> other members of her study group, they urged her to help unite
> the two families. With much patient effort she finally brought
> the families together to talk it over. Each said that they bore
> part of the responsibility and the misunderstanding was cleared
> up.[4]

It is through the mechanism of study groups (*hsueh hsi hsiao
tsu*) that the attempt is being made to teach the entire population a different way of relating to their world, to "remold their
world outlook," as the Chinese say. It is in these study groups,
in the factories, in the neighborhoods, and in the schools, that
the Chinese citizen is encouraged to think scientifically about
the world around him, to attempt to put aside superstition and
"subjective reality" in favor of "objective reality." It is in the
study group, surrounded by co-workers or neighbors, that he is
expected to examine himself honestly, his attitudes and be-

havior, and attempt to evaluate whether he is still motivated by self-interest and individualism or whether he is attempting to contribute to the common good. These meetings are punctuated by bouts of "criticism and self-criticism" as members struggle to function within their society according to current norms.

Study groups are thus the mechanism through which new policies and programs are communicated to the vast mass of the Chinese people and the vehicle by which these new policies are adapted to the local work unit, the residents' committee, or the individual. For example, toward the end of the Cultural Revolution, once again the emphasis was placed on raising production. Individual work units would receive the word to "promote production"; it would then be their responsibility to think through in their study groups ways of implementing this new thrust. How can our unit work more effectively? Are there improvements that can be made in the machinery we use to increase production? Can we reallocate manpower to maximize production? These are the kinds of questions that might be raised in local groups once the larger policy has been set at a higher level.

These small study groups are characterized by a level of intimacy rarely shared in urban America outside of, perhaps, therapy groups. As one American who has lived in China for many years has observed, "Study groups are composed of people with whom you work every day or of neighbors whose life is intimately linked with your own. . . . Everyone is well versed in the others' personalities, traits and expressions, and this makes the atmosphere for criticism and self-criticism a little easier."[5]

This intimacy and interdependence continues outside of study groups and pervades much of Chinese life. And, of course, the relative lack of mobility of the vast majority of China's citizens means that in all likelihood one would continue to live and work with the same group of people. There is little moving on to the next job or the next city if this situation doesn't work out. This comparative permanence undoubtedly contributes to the feelings of intimacy and to the willingness to interact on a personal level that many of us, in our mobile lives with our throwaway relationships, would be unwilling to tolerate. Perhaps Liu Ju-chin, of the Brick Tower Residents' Committee, illustrates most vividly the interrelatedness of families in the urban courtyard and the attempt to utilize all talents, to discard no one even if he is elderly, sick, or burdened down with his own responsibilities:

> Sun Fu-lun, living at No. 27 in a courtyard of six families, doesn't go out to work because she has a number of children to take care of. All the husbands and wives in the other five families go out to work, and when their children come home from school there is usually no one home. So Sun Fu-lun has boiled water on hand for the children to drink and helps them to do things like prepare meals and buy groceries. Her grateful neighbors do all they can after work to help her with her household chores, and knit sweaters for her children in spare moments. Coming from different places and working at different jobs, the six families did not know each other before, but now they feel very close to each other. Since Sun Fu-lun is always at home, the other families leave their keys with her and she has become the yard's "housekeeper."[6]

Sian

In the Lian Hu district of Sian off North Street bustling with shops and shoppers, trucks, buses, and bicycles is Ching Nian Lu, a quiet, narrow street with gray-brick walls along both sides. Young trees whitewashed halfway up have been planted every few feet in the dust on the side of the road. At Number 62 Ching Nian Lu a gray-brick one-room building trimmed in bright blue serves as the headquarters for the residents' committee. One wall is decorated with pictures of Marx, Engels, Lenin, and Stalin; a larger picture of Mao Tse-tung hangs on the opposite wall.

Seated around a long conference table were representatives from the city commune who are responsible for this residents' committee, representatives of the residents' committee itself, and the head of the Ching Nian Lu Residents' Committee, Ho Kuei-lan. Comrade Ho is a fifty-one-year-old plump woman with a smooth face, a small, shy voice, and a frightened manner. Her dark hair is parted in the middle with two gray streaks in front. Comrade Ho spoke of the work of the residents' committee, referring often to notes held in her shaking hands.

"The residents' committee," Comrade Ho began, "is a mass organization. It is made up of nine members—one chairman, two vice-chairmen, and six group leaders. Our main task is to run the welfare work for the people who live here. As part of this welfare work, we have a health station with five Red Medical Workers. They take care of minor illnesses, health education, and birth control for the families in this area. In addition to health work we take care of the life of the residents in this area. If, for example, a widow with no children becomes ill, we help her to find a doctor and help her to buy grain or perhaps coal. Or if both parents are at work and there is no one to look after the old people in the home, we help to look after them. We organize groups of children after school and on holidays and organize activities for them such as singing songs, reading books, physical activities, and cultural activities."

Comrade Ho, gaining confidence, her voice becoming firmer, continued: "We also send the requests and demands of the masses to the higher-level committee. When the housewives wanted to go to work, their requests were sent to the commune level, and factories were organized. Now the housewives play an important role in making production for the country. Sometimes people have difficulties with their living conditions. For example, the running water tap may be too close to a family's home and may be too noisy. The family can then request to have it moved. Or if a road is damaged, the masses will report this to the residents' committee who will in turn report it to the cadres at the commune level; they will report it to the city level." In answer to a query about how long it would take for the road to be repaired, Comrade Ho replied that it would be repaired within one week. "The high-level committee pays much attention to these matters!" Ho Kuei-lan said with feeling.

"The third task of the residents' committee is to mobilize the masses to fulfill the tasks handed down by the higher level of the government. In the summer and fall the people take part in the Patriotic Sanitation Campaign under the direction of the residents' committee. [The Patriotic Sanitation Campaign, which originated in the early 1950's, mobilized the general population to combat infectious disease, and to exterminate flies, mosquitoes, rats, and sparrows. Sparrows were later replaced by bedbugs. It has been continued over the past two decades and encourages popular participation in health care and periodic neighborhood cleanup campaigns.] People also carry out specific tasks handed down by the city commune. Chairman Mao told us to plant more trees in order to make the surroundings more beautiful and to make everything green. The commune gives the people trees to plant; they then plant them along the street and in the courtyard and take care of them.

"We also organize the masses in the city to support the autumn harvest. Some people will go out to the countryside and help with the harvest. Students and workers in the commune factories go out for a few weeks, but they continue to receive their salary from the factory. And in the spring we send fertilizer to the countryside to support agriculture."

Ho Kuei-lan has been head of the residents' committee since it was formed in 1958, and prior to that she had been active in

neighborhood activities for many years. In the early 1950's she
organized literacy classes for housewives, and she herself
"studied hard." Comrade Ho's husband, Wang Wen-kuan, is in
his fifties but looks considerably older. He has a stubble of a
beard, his hands are nicotine-stained, and he speaks slowly and
haltingly. He and Comrade Ho were married in 1941. He worked
as a shoemaker and as a part-time cadre in the residents' committee until recently when the workers in the Ching Nian Lu
Commune Incense Factory asked him to become its director
because they felt that he was especially able at working together
with other units. Now he works only at the incense factory but
earns the same salary he did at his previous job, fifty yuan per
month. Comrade Ho and Comrade Wang have one son, a
twenty-six-year-old factory worker who currently lives in
Kwangtung province.

Comrade Ho estimated that she spends about six hours a day,
six days a week, on her work with the residents' committee.
For this she receives a small stipend of eighteen yuan per
month. Since she was elected head in 1958, she has been re-
elected every two years. The two vice-chairmen, however, were
elected during the most recent election in May, 1971.

The residents' committee is divided into six groups, each
with a group leader. An Fu-kuei lives at Number 50 Ching Nian
Lu and is the group leader for Group No. IV, which encom-
passes six courtyards along Ching Nian Lu. One hundred and
eighty people live in these six courtyards. Comrade An, an
elderly, slightly deaf man with a beard and a moustache, wearing a gray-blue Mao shirt, greeted visitors at the door of his
one-room house by shaking hands and bowing slightly from the
waist. He was born seventy years ago here in Sian. "Before
Liberation," according to Comrade An, "we had a hard life, and
even though I had steady work, we did not have enough to eat.
Since Liberation I have worked for many years in a machine-

tool factory and retired seven years ago." Comrade An receives a pension of forty yuan per month, 70 percent of his former salary.

He lives with his sixty-three-year-old wife and twelve-year-old grandson. He and his wife have three daughters, all of whom live in Sian. The youngest daughter is a primary-school teacher in a suburb to the north, and it is one of her children who lives, and has lived since infancy, with his grandparents. Her two other children live at home, and she comes once a week to visit this child.

Comrade An said that one of his jobs as a group leader is to "organize the masses to study." Out of the 180 people in his six courtyards, only 31, 30 housewives and 1 retired worker, are at home full-time and therefore do not belong to a group elsewhere. Comrade An commented that all of the housewives are older women, as all the young women of Ching Nian Lu work. He meets together with the 31 residents every Tuesday and Friday afternoons from 2:30 to 4:30. The two or three residents who are literate will take turns reading the Sian *Daily* aloud, and then everyone will discuss the content and meaning of what has been read. They also discuss the sanitation work that needs to be done.

Chang Chung-hsiu, a kind-looking elderly man in a black jacket who smokes his cigarettes with a cigarette holder, also emphasized his work in organizing the people to study and to read newspapers. All the groups in the residents' committee meet at the same time on Tuesdays and Fridays (the chairman visits various groups, rotating among them). Comrade Chang's group also holds literacy classes; those who know how to read and write teach the rest. They study Mao's "Three Constantly Read Articles" ("Serve the People," "In Memory of Norman Bethune," and "The Foolish Old Man Who Removed the Mountains"), which Comrade Chang felt are "easy for the masses to understand." In addition they study somewhat longer, more complex essays of Mao's, "On Contradiction" and "Combat Liberalism."

Chang Chung-hsiu also spoke of his efforts to mediate disputes. Though he felt that there are not too many problems to be solved among the residents, he allowed that there were a few. When pressed for an example of his mediation efforts, he told the following story:

"A worker's family who lived at Number Eighteen Ching Nian Lu had a fifteen-year-old son, Chu Mao-mao, a middle-school student. Chu Mao-mao wanted to make a trip back to his family's native province, and his father gave him thirteen yuan to buy a train ticket.

"Chu Mao-mao was very happy and went to the railroad station to buy his ticket, but he lost the money on the way. Another child, Liu Hsi-ting, nine years old, who lived in Number Twenty Ching Nian Lu, found the money on the road. He tried to find out whose money it was; he went to several courtyards but could not find the owner.

"Meanwhile Chu Mao-mao returned home very sad. First he told his family that he had lost the money; then he came to me and told me about the money. Soon after, Liu Hsi-ting told me he had found some money. I brought them together, and Liu Hsi-ting asked Chu Mao-mao how much he had lost and how many bills he had had. Chu Mao-mao told him, 'Thirteen yuan in nine notes.' Since this is exactly what the younger child had found, he returned the money to Chu Mao-mao, who was very happy."

Several points are particularly revealing about Comrade Chang's story: first, that even though the two boys live only two courtyards apart, and people generally know one another and one another's problems extremely well in China's neighborhoods, they still did not connect with each other without the aid

of the group leader; second, a corollary to the first, the clear
advantage of having a neutral trusted person to be able to turn
to in a time of trouble; and third, Comrade Chang's encouraging the boy who found the money to check Chu Mao-mao on
the exact amount and number of bills before returning it.
Though people are expected to be honest, precautions are nevertheless taken to ensure such honesty. Informal mediation has,
of course, been favored in China for centuries. As Jerome Alan
Cohen has pointed out, "For millennia the Chinese have preferred unofficial mediation to official adjudication."[7] After the
overthrow of the Manchu dynasty the republican government
attempted to enact legislation to institutionalize extrajudicial
mediation and in 1913 created a Commercial Arbitration Bureau to mediate commercial disputes. The Nationalist government further attempted to modernize traditional mediation
techniques, and the Communist government "made popular
mediation a major instrument of its legal policy."[8]

Local mediators and mediation committees have taken on
added importance with the paucity of laws enacted during the
decade between the Great Leap Forward (1958) and the Great
Proletarian Cultural Revolution (1966–1969). They, along
with study groups, newspaper editorials, radio broadcasts, and
local governments, have been key in communicating norms to
China's people. Study groups have been a particularly important socializing force. As Victor Li points out:

> The Chinese have undertaken a vigorous and thorough pro-
> gram of public legal education. With the exception of young
> children, everyone is a member of one or more "small groups"
> which are composed of about twenty persons who are closely
> affiliated through their employment, place of residence, or
> other ties. In addition to other activities, those groups engage
> in a number of hours of "study" each week; a substantial por-
> tion of the study sessions deal with matters falling under the

rubric of law.... Moreover, an effort is made to apply the
general principles examined to the actual living and working
conditions of the members of the group.[9]

Not only is the study group instrumental in communicating
the law or current norms to the general population, but it is also
key in enforcing those norms. Li points out that group members
know one another so well that incipient antisocial behavior can
be spotted early and dealt with immediately. It is considered
one's responsibility to help one's neighbor or one's co-worker
correct deviations in thought or in behavior:

> If a person truly loves his neighbor or truly is his brother's
> keeper, then he has a moral and social duty to correct his
> brother's shortcomings. If truly no man is an island and the
> actions of each person directly affect the lives of all others, then
> the "group," however defined, has a real and direct stake in
> controlling the actions of its members.[10]

Thus local leaders such as Chang Chung-hsiu and Ho Kuei-lan
become extremely important in the functioning of Chinese
society.

Comrade Chang has been a group leader only since May,
1971. Though he was born here in Shensi province, he worked
as a cadre for eleven years in Tsinghai province in the northwest. Because he developed heart disease, he retired early in
1966, returned to Sian, and has since been living at Number 18.
Comrade Chang's wife is a worker in a printing and binding
factory nearby, and his three children are in school—two in
middle school and a twelve-year-old in primary school. According to Comrade Chang, "Because I am sick and old, we all have
to help each other. The children help each other, and they help
me. And I do some of the cooking while they help with the
washing." And yet while Comrade Chang himself needs help

from his family, he is helping others. He seemed neither old nor sick as he told the story of Chu Mao-mao and his thirteen yuan; he seemed vital and alive and needed.

In the same fashion, when Ho Kuei-lan told about resolving marital disputes, she came alive, her face brightened, and her voice became firmer: "If a couple is quarreling, a member of the residents' committee will go to the home and advise the couple to unite." And then one of the vice-chairmen, Chang Chieh-sheng, an elderly man with a warm manner and smile lines around his eyes, his dark blue cap on the back of his head, added, "If a couple is quarreling, the children, sometimes even children of eight or nine, will come to the residents' committee to ask for help. Whoever is available will go. We will talk separately with the husband and with the wife and then all talk together. If the children are at home, they will attend, and if older people live in the home, they may attend, too."

If the marital problems persist and the couple wish to request a divorce, they must go to see a "cadre of basic state power" in the Administrative Office of the Ching Nian commune. This cadre is a man about forty years old without any special training but one who has a "good knowledge of the Chinese Marriage Law and of party policy." According to members of the committee, this cadre has "more experience with this kind of work" and "is good with other people's problems." He will first ask the couple their reason for wanting a divorce; he will then "try his best to advise them to unite, not to separate." He will talk with members of their working units and consult with members of their residents' committee. He will then meet with the marital partners separately, then together—often three to five times and sometimes even as many as ten times.

If the couple still wish a divorce, they will then simply obtain a certificate from this same cadre. Out of 9,100 families in the Ching Nian commune from January to September, 1972, seventeen couples requested divorces. Six couples were "united," and the remaining eleven, whose "characters and feelings were different," received divorces.

Similarly, if a couple wish to marry, they go to the Administrative Office of the commune. After they are asked their age and if either has been married before, they are issued a certificate that states that they are married. Representatives from both the residents' committee and the commune stressed that if all is in compliance with the Chinese Marriage Law, they always give the certificate. Since part of the current massive birth-control efforts include urging young women to delay marriage until they are twenty-four to twenty-six, and men until they are twenty-six to twenty-nine, the question was raised about what action the Administrative Office would take if a boy of twenty-two and a girl of nineteen wished to marry. The response was that they would urge them to wait but that if the couple insisted, they would receive their marriage certificate. They elaborated by saying that most women living in the Ching Nian Lu commune marry around the age of twenty-three and most men around twenty-four or twenty-five.

The Ching Nian Lu Residents' Committee also helps with other human problems. If a person dies and had been working, the work unit will help the family to settle his affairs. If the deceased was a housewife or a retired worker, the family will manage their affairs without help if possible, but if they need help, the residents' committee will send someone to the house to help with "concrete problems and with feelings."

The committee also helps the disabled to find appropriate work. It has helped five deaf and dumb people, after they had graduated from a special school, to find jobs. One became a carpenter, two went to work in the metal factory, and the other two in the printing and binding factory run by the commune. Comrade Ho stressed that these individuals have chosen this work and that the residents' committee would find other work for them if the jobs were too difficult.

Although the residents' committee is heavily involved in helping residents when such help is needed, the expectation seems to be that families will take care of one another, within the context of full employment (for men, at least), decent housing, at least a minimum income, and essentials kept at artificially low prices. Members of the committees do not rush to help with each crisis; it seemed, rather, that families were expected to work out their own problems but that these committee members were available when they were needed. While China is a society where many basic necessities are guaranteed, it is simultaneously a society that places a heavy responsibility on the individual to work out his own problems whenever possible, to help family, friends, and neighbors with their problems, and to be informed about and contribute to that society.

NOTES

[1] Felix Greene, *China* (New York: Ballantine Books, 1962), p. 206.

[2] Liu Ju-chin, "Study Brings a Broader View," *China Reconstructs*, Vol. XXII, No. 8 (August, 1973), p. 7.

[3] *Ibid.*

[4] *Ibid.*

[5] Gerald Tannebaum, speech delivered at the Forum on Technology and Social Change, Iowa State University, Ames, Iowa, October 4, 1973.

[6] Liu Ju-chin, *loc. cit.*

[7] Jerome Alan Cohen, "Drafting People's Mediation Rules," in John Wilson Lewis, ed., *The City in Communist China* (Stanford, Calif.: Stanford University Press, 1971), p. 29.

[8] *Ibid.*, p. 30.

[9] Victor H. Li, "Law and Penology: Systems of Reform and Correction," in Michel Oksenberg, ed., *China's Developmental Experience*, New York, Columbia University, *Proceedings of the Academy of Political Science*, Vol. XXXI, No. 1 (March, 1973), p. 150.

[10] *Ibid.*, p. 151.

THE SUNG FAMILY

Sung Kwang-chen is a fifty-four-year-old woman with a long thin oval face. She and her husband, her seventy-six-year-old mother-in-law, her seventeen-year-old daughter, her married daughter, son-in-law, and three-and-a-half-year-old grandson live in their small three-room house in a courtyard of the Fengsheng Neighborhood. The front room of the house is decorated with plants and lace curtains at the windows, a map of China on one wall, pictures of the family on another. Sitting in this simple room with its whitewashed walls and stone floors, a few toys scattered around—a helicopter, a doll, a car—a tiny black and white kitten playing outside the door, Comrade Sung tells about her life. "Before Liberation we were very poor. My husband's father worked for a landlord in Hupei province. He died at the age of twenty-six, leaving two children both very young, one a year old and the other, my husband, just a few months old. My mother-in-law took care of the two children, but when they became thirteen, they had to find work. It was very difficult to find work at that time, and my husband did not have enough to eat.

"After Liberation people were able to get work regularly, and my husband started working in a factory here in Peking twenty-three years ago. I came to Peking to be with him eighteen years ago and worked in a factory until recently when I stopped because of ill health. In the past there was no medical care or medicine when people were ill; now the lane health station is there to help the people, and the Red Medical Workers come to the house to take care of you if you are sick. Before we were so very poor, and now we have a sewing machine, a radio, and every member of the family who works has a watch."

The family is crowded in its small house: Comrade Sung's mother-in-law, her small grandson, and her seventeen-year-old daughter, a teacher in a primary school, share one bedroom; she and her husband share a second bedroom; and her daughter, thirty, a saleswoman in a local shop, and her son-in-law, a factory worker in another district of Peking, share the third bedroom. They have two other children who are not living at home, a son, twenty-six, a factory worker in another city, and a daughter, twenty-one, who is also a factory worker and lives in a dormitory here in Peking.

Comrade Sung proudly told of how the family is now able to save money in the bank. The total family income is 206 yuan per month, food costs 150 yuan for the entire family, and rent, electricity, and water together come to 12 yuan per month. But what seemed even more important to Comrade Sung was that if she became ill, the residents' committee would arrange a car to bring her to the neighborhood hospital, and if she needed to, she could even go to a higher-level hospital.

CHAPTER 4

NEIGHBORHOOD HEALTH CARE

> The main task of our hospital is to give
> medical care to the residents of this neigh-
> borhood.
>
> —Liu Pei-pung, director of the
> Fengsheng Neighborhood Hospital

THE CHARACTERIZATION of China in the first half of this century as the "Sick Man of Asia" was largely used metaphorically.
It referred to China's technological backwardness, its inability
to feed its people or provide them with other necessities of life,
and its defenselessness in the face of economic and military
onslaughts from the technologically developed nations. Although in its metaphorical sense this characteristic may have
been overstated, in a literal sense China's sickness was very
deep indeed. The country was plagued with almost every known
form of nutritional and infectious disease, including cholera,
leprosy, tuberculosis, typhoid fever, beriberi, scurvy, and
plague. Venereal disease was widespread. One observer has estimated that China suffered four million "unnecessary" deaths
each year.

To have some conception of the transformation that has been
wrought in China's cities, one must first have a glimpse of the
conditions under which people lived twenty-five short years ago.
According to Theodore H. White and Annalee Jacoby, reporters
in China during World War II:

> The cities reeked of opium; cholera, dysentery, syphilis, and
> trachoma rotted the health of the people . . . sewage and gar-

bage were emptied into the same stream from which drinking
water was taken. . . . Dust coated the city [Chungking] almost
as thickly as mud during the wintertime. Moisture remained in
the air, perspiration dripped, and prickly heat ravaged the
skin. Every errand became an expedition, each expedition an
ordeal. Swarms of bugs emerged; small green ones swam on
drinking water, and spiders four inches across crawled on the
walls. The famous Chungking mosquitoes came, and Americans
claimed the mosquitoes worked in threes; two lifted the mos-
quito net, while the third zoomed in for the kill. Meat spoiled;
there was never enough water for washing; dysentery spread
and could not be evaded.[1]

Rewi Alley, a New Zealander who has lived for many years
in China, describes child laborers in a light-bulb factory:

There are nine factories in the immediate vicinity of this one,
each packed to capacity with child workers amongst whom skin
diseases, such as scabies and great festering legs due primarily
to bed bug bites, are very common. I was especially struck by
the bad condition of two little boys whose beri-beri swollen
legs were covered with running sores, and whose tired little
bodies slumped wearily against the bench after they have
moved to answer my questions.[2]

In addition to the cruel poverty under which the Chinese
people lived, which created some and exacerbated most of their
health problems, there existed a woefully inadequate number
of medical personnel and hospital facilities. And most of what
did exist were centered in and around the urban areas. Thus,
when the Communists took power in 1949, one of their first
priorities was the provision of more adequate medical care. At
a National Health Congress in Peking in the early 1950's four
principles were adopted, which remain the foundation on which
medical policy is determined:

1. Medicine must serve the workers, peasants, and soldiers (*gong-nong-bing*).

2. Preventive medicine must be given priority over curative medicine.

3. Practitioners of Chinese traditional medicine must be united with practitioners of Western medicine.

4. Health work must be integrated with mass movements.

This last principle is of great importance because the Chinese leaders recognized that the great mass of the Chinese people had to be educated about health—about sanitation, infectious disease, venereal disease, principles of public health—for a revolution in health to take place. They recognized that a dramatic change in the health care of China's vast population could not be superimposed from above. And so they set about involving people in their own health care.

The mobilization of the masses has been the primary technique by which the Chinese have accomplished their feats of engineering: the construction of their canals, bridges, large-scale irrigation projects, and dikes and the damming of rivers. The mobilization of the masses has been the primary mechanism in their feats of human engineering also. Han Suyin describes the process of education of the masses since 1949 as one that has included the "eradication of the feudal mind" and "getting the masses away from the anchored belief that natural calamities are 'fixed by heaven' and that therefore nothing can be done to remedy one's lot." She continues: "To bridge this gap between scientific modern man and feudal man, the prey of superstition, and to do it within the compass of one generation, is a formidable task."[3] One of the prime techniques used to accomplish this "formidable task" has been the activating of the people. In health care this has meant the broadest involvement of people at every level of society in movements such as the Great Patriotic Health Campaign. It has also meant the recruitment from the population they are to serve of selected groups of people such as barefoot doctors, peasants who are given short periods of training and then return to their communes to do agricultural work part-time and medical work part-time, Red Medical Workers in the cities, and worker-doctors in the factories. The individual has been mobilized as well to "fight against his own disease."

As Mao Tse-tung stated in his essay "On Practice" in 1937:

> If you want knowledge, you must take part in the practice of changing reality. If you want to know the taste of a pear, you must change the pear by eating it yourself. If you want to know the structure and properties of the atom, you must make physical and chemical experiments to change the state of the atom. If you want to know the theory and methods of revolution, you must take part in revolution. All genuine knowledge originates in direct experience.[4]

During the first decade and a half of Communist rule unprecedented changes took place in the health and health-care system of China. Cholera, plague, smallpox, and most nutritional illnesses quickly disappeared; opium addiction was eliminated, largely through community-based efforts; venereal disease took somewhat longer, but through a combination of social and medical techniques was reportedly almost completely wiped out in most of China by the early 1960's. Through the Great Patriotic Health Movements, the people were mobilized against the "four pests": flies, mosquitoes, rats, and bedbugs. As the process was described in 1971, "old customs and habits of the people were changed," "society was remolded," and "a new social attitude of 'regarding hygiene as an honor' took root among the mass of our people."[5]

Health-care personnel were trained at an astonishing rate. It is estimated that over 100,000 doctors were trained in less than twenty years and large numbers of assistant doctors, nurses, midwives, pharmacists, and radiology and laboratory technicians as well. During the Cultural Revolution the Chinese medical establishment was severely criticized despite these incredible advances that had taken place during the first fifteen years of Communist rule.

Mao Tse-tung singled out the Ministry of Health for criticism in a statement made on June 26, 1965. In his statement Mao urged a shorter period of time for medical education, that more time and effort be devoted toward "the prevention and the improved treatment of common diseases," and particularly castigated the medical establishment for neglecting the needs of people in the countryside. The final sentence of the statement, which has come to be known as simply the "June 26 Directive," is: "In medical and health work, put the stress on the rural areas!"[6] Since the Cultural Revolution China has attempted to redress the balance between medical care provided for those in the cities and medical care in the countryside. Far greater numbers of paraprofessionals have been developed, particularly barefoot doctors in the rural areas. These paraprofessionals are people recruited from among the "mass" who are given short periods of training, not long enough to alienate them from their peer group, and then sent back to give first-level medical care. In the cities the health workers at the local level are former housewives who have been trained to be Red Medical Workers. Three of them serve the fifteen hundred people who live in the Wu Ting Residents' Committee, located in the western part of the Fengsheng Neighborhood. The chairman of the residents' committee, Chao Huan-ching, serves as the director of the Wu Ting Residents' Committee Health Station, although he is not himself a health worker.

The major functions of a residents' committee health station are preventive work, the treatment of minor illness, health education, and sanitation work. In Wu Ting the station is located in a single room off one of the courtyards. Its fairly typical equipment includes a bed for examination or treatment, a table with chairs at which consultations may occur (or tea shared with American visitors), and a cabinet with both Western-type and traditional Chinese medicines. On the walls are a picture of Mao Tse-tung, an acupuncture chart, and health-education posters.

One of Wu Ting's Red Medical Workers, Comrade Yang Hsio-hua, is thirty-eight years old. After her marriage she worked briefly as a saleswoman until age nineteen, when her first child was born. Since then she has been home taking care of her children, now ages nineteen, fifteen, and eleven. Two years ago, responding to a call to "Serve the People," which grew out of the Cultural Revolution, she volunteered for one month of training in the Fengsheng Neighborhood Hospital. During the training period she and her fellow house-wives learned history-taking and simple physical-examination techniques, such as blood-pressure determination. They were taught the uses of a number of Western and herb medicines and techniques of acupuncture and of intramuscular and subcutaneous injection. Preventive measures, such as sanitation, immunization, and birth-control techniques, were an important part of the curriculum. But the most important part, according to Comrade Yang, was that she and her colleagues were taught that there are no barriers between them and the acquisition of medical knowledge other than their own fears. Once these are overcome, in part by sessions in which the "bitter past" and the feelings of the students are shared and discussed, the house-wives feel it is indeed possible to become medical personnel. Comrade Yang continues to learn from a doctor from the neighborhood hospital who visits the residents' committee health station three times a week, from her own periodic visits to the hospital about a patient or for instruction, and from the bi-weekly or monthly meetings of all the Red Medical Workers of the neighborhood.

Another Red Medical Worker of Wu Ting is Comrade Chang Cheng-yu, a forty-three-year-old mother of two children, ages twenty-one and twelve. She has been a housewife all her married life and never worked outside the home until she became a health worker. Both Comrade Yang and Comrade Chang live in the residents' committee area within a few steps of the health station. The station is staffed by them and their colleagues from 8:00 A.M. to 11:00 A.M., when they usually see seven to ten patients, and from 3:00 P.M. to 5:30 P.M., when they see four or five additional patients. If the patient does not feel well during the times when the health station is closed, the patient can go directly to the home of one of the Red Medical Workers, although this evidently happens rather rarely.

The health workers are paid a modest sum for their work, about fifteen yuan per month, roughly one-third the wages of a beginning factory worker. These wages come in part from the small payments made by patients visiting the health station, in part from the collective income from the neighborhood factories, and in part from the home embroidery industry. The fee paid for a patient visit to the health station is never more than ten fen (four cents), and usually far less. If the patient is a retired worker, he or she may present the bills from the health station to the former factory, where reimbursement is made in full. If the patient is a dependent of someone who is now working or a retired worker, the factory will reimburse half the health-station charge. People who are currently working are rarely seen in residents' committee health stations because their primary medical-care needs are taken care of at their place of work.

A large part of the duties of the Red Medical Worker, under the supervision of the Department of Public Health of the neighborhood hospital, relates to sanitation work in the neighborhood. As part of the Great Patriotic Health Campaign there are ongoing campaigns particularly in the summer against flies and mosquitoes, and attempts are made to prevent the spread of gastrointestinal disease. The entire population is mobilized under the supervision of the Red Medical Workers to keep the neighborhood clean, with special cleanup days set aside, especially around the May 1 and October 1 celebrations. In the winter and spring the health workers are concerned mainly with the prevention of upper respiratory infections, for which they encourage morning exercises, washing of the face with cold water, long walks, the use of traditional medicines, and when a patient has a cold, the use of masks to prevent its spread. Some health stations organize mass meetings and study groups to educate the people about infectious disease; people are taught to report all infectious disease to the health station immediately.

The Public Health Department also supervises the Red Medical Workers in providing immunizations. These are usually given in the residents' committee health station. The Red Medical Workers will often go to the homes to bring the children to the health station for immunization, and if it is necessary for some reason, may give the immunization in the home. It is considered the responsibility of the health workers as well as that of the parents to make sure that all those eligible for immunizations are, in actuality, immunized. Perhaps it is this mutual feeling of responsibility on the part of both the citizen and the health establishment that accounts for the incredible immunization rate and subsequent drop in infectious disease in China.

The Red Medical Workers also have as their responsibility the provision of birth-control information. They give out oral contraceptives directly, often with no specific medical examination prior to initiation of treatment. Intrauterine contraceptive devices are available, and insertion is performed by trained personnel in the neighborhood hospital. The Red Medical Workers make periodic visits to all of the women of the residents' committee area encouraging the use of contraception and discussing with them the need to lower China's birth rate and the importance of "plannned birth" in the liberation of women. If women are burdened by bearing and caring for many children, they say, they cannot be part of society and make their contribution to the society.

The Red Medical Workers also care for patients with "minor illnesses" and provide follow-up care after a patient has been treated in a hospital. For example, one day Red Medical Workers were treating patients with arthritis using a combination of acupuncture and herb medicine and were also checking blood pressures in patients with hypertension to determine the appropriate dose of medication. The therapy for these patients had been started in the neighborhood or district hospital and the continuing dose of medication prescribed there. The Red Medical Worker may herself change the type of traditional medicine given to a hypertensive patient, but can vary the dose of Western medicine only within certain limits. If the patient's blood pressure is found to be outside the limits set by the hospital, the patient is sent back to the hospital for treatment and new instructions.

The Min Kang Residents' Committee also has three Red Medical Workers to care for its housewives, retired workers, and children. In the small one-room health station two health workers were seeing patients one autumn morning. Yang Kuo-ying, a heavy woman in her fifties, describes her symptoms and her medical care: "I have had high blood pressure since nineteen sixty. In the past I used traditional medicine, but when I felt faint, I went to the hospital, and they gave me Western medicine. Now I come here for the Western medicine which the hospital prescribes and for traditional medicine which the Red Medical Worker prescribes. If my blood pressure rises, I will return to the hospital." Comrade Yang goes to the health station once a week to have her temperature taken and her pressure checked and to receive her medicine at a cost of three fen, which she pays herself.

Chen Wen-ching is a fifty-two-year-old housewife who complains of an ache in her arm. She thinks it may be an inflammation and has had it for seven or eight months. "First I went to the Fengsheng Neighborhood Hospital, and the doctor gave me medicine for injections," she recounted, sitting on an examining table with her legs dangling off the side. "I buy the medicine [vitamin B_1 and vitamin B_{12}] at the hospital for two yuan, bring it here, and have the injections here. I have had one daily for several months, plus acupuncture, and feel my arm is getting better. It is very convenient for me to come here, as I live right nearby." It costs Comrade Chen three fen for each visit to the health station.

The backup institution for these two residents' committees is the Fengsheng Neighborhood Hospital. This hospital is built around two large courtyards, both with dirt floors. Patients wait for their appointment in the courtyard sitting on benches that are scattered amid the trees and bushes. A wooden roof covers part of the main courtyard in case of rain; bicycles stand parked on one side, bamboo strollers on another. At nine o'clock in the morning few people are waiting, but by midmorning there are perhaps as many as twenty-five or thirty.

Mrs. Liu Pei-pung, the director of the hospital, looks to be about fifty and wears glasses, the traditional pants, gray jacket, and light blue blouse. With a ready smile and a competent manner she describes the people served by the hospital: "Although there are twenty-five residents' committees in the Fengsheng Neighborhood, this hospital only serves eleven residents' committees, five thousand families who make up a population of twenty thousand. Fifteen hundred preschool children are included in the population served in addition to the children who attend four primary schools and two middle schools. We also take care of the employees of five factories."

Mrs. Liu continues, "Twenty-seven doctors—twenty traditional doctors and seven Western-trained doctors—thirty-one nurses and technicians, and thirty-two other personnel treat about eight hundred patients daily. Some of the staff worked in private clinics before Liberation, and some of them have come directly from medical college. There is no ward here; the patients must go elsewhere for hospitalization. But we have seven departments—the department of medicine, surgery, traditional bone disease, acupuncture, gynecology, dentistry, and tuberculosis. We also have four assistant departments—a pharmacy including both traditional Chinese medicines and Western medicines, a laboratory, an X-ray department, and an injection department."

The neighborhood hospital has trained 204 Red Medical Workers to give medical care and health education in the residents' committees. Mrs. Liu declared emphatically, "The main task of our hospital is to give medical care to the residents of this neighborhood. When epidemics occur, the doctors of this hospital go to the residents' committee to help the Red Medical Workers. They also train the Red Medical Workers and direct their work. Minor diseases can be treated in lower-level clinics by Red Medical Workers, as this is more convenient for the people. But if they cannot treat the illness, the patient will be referred here. The Red Medical Worker," Mrs. Liu continued, "usually uses traditional Chinese medicines which they have collected themselves. This is not only extremely convenient but the price is very low also."

As part of the effort made to make medical care available to the residents of the neighborhood, a doctor from the neighborhood hospital will make a home visit to any patient suffering from an acute illness. Furthermore, if a retired military man or a retired worker is ill, a doctor will make a special effort to visit him in his home.

Referral to a higher-level hospital and consultation from a higher-level hospital are frequently and readily available. Just as the doctors in the neighborhood hospital consult with the Red Medical Workers, so do doctors from a higher-level hospital consult weekly with the neighborhood hospital physicians. Moreover, Red Medical Workers refer patients they cannot deal with to the neighborhood hospital, and physicians at the neighborhood hospital refer patients they cannot deal with to the higher-level hospitals.

The Department of Public Health is a key unit within the Neighborhood Hospital. Dr. Chi Li-hua, a woman who looked to be in her mid-forties with a ruddy oval face, short dark hair tucked behind her ears, and a gray-blue jacket, described the activities of her department: "Our main task is to educate the people about prevention. We work primarily on giving immunizations, on the management of infectious disease, on the health of children, on family planning, and on the management of occupational diseases in the factories. We also work on wiping out the 'four pests' and on teaching the people the importance of sanitation. We put up blackboards with health-education messages on them, and we put up pictures of the four pests and of bacteria in order to educate people. For we think that people can more easily understand health issues through concrete propaganda; if the people know the importance of these matters, they will cooperate.

"We also are responsible for the health conditions within the restaurants in our neighborhood. We check to make sure that all utensils are clean and that the food is properly handled. The Municipal Bureau of Public Health makes public-health policy and inspects the facilities, and the local districts implement the policy."

Immunizations are given to children in the neighborhood jointly by a public-health doctor and a Red Medical Worker. The Fengsheng Neighborhood Hospital has an astonishing record of children immunized. The percentages of children immunized out of the total number eligible during the period January to September, 1972, are as follows:

Smallpox	86.9%
Tuberculosis	92.1%
Diphtheria, pertussis, tetanus	95.8%
Measles	99.6%
Poliomyelitis	93.8%
Meningococcal meningitis	94.2%
Epidemic encephalitis	96.0%

The public-health doctors were very concerned about the management of infectious disease. According to Dr. Chi, "When we get a report of measles, we keep the patient at home, and we worry about the health of the children in the same courtyard. If the children have been vaccinated, it is all right, but if not, we make sure that they are vaccinated. The measles patient herself remains at home until she is well. If a patient gets diarrhea, we recommend separate eating utensils and urge the use of disinfectants to the stools and the use of disinfectants in the homes of these patients.

"We put great stress on the health of both women and children. If women have too many children, it is not good for the woman's health. The Red Medical Doctors are very clear on the number of children that each family has and bring birth-control medications to the family free." Dr. Chi emphasized that each family could choose whatever method they preferred and that the Red Medical Workers emphasized education in birth control. The birth rate of the population in the Fengsheng Neighborhood is eighteen per thousand. Dr. Chi, discussing birth control further, commented, "If women work, they only want to have two or three children; even housewives only want two or three children."

The hospital is administered by a "leading group" or "revolutionary committee" of five members, all women, including Comrade Liu and Yang Lan-ying, the administrative officer, both of whom are full-time members. The three other members are part-time and have other jobs as well—one is a nurse, one works in the pharmacy, and one is a traditional Chinese doctor. The group meets at least once a week to plan the medical work and to "study how to better serve the people." They listen to the complaints of both doctors and patients. If some doctors feel there are too many patients, the leading group "organizes the doctors into study groups and helps them to change their attitudes." If a patient has a special request such as wanting a doctor to make a home visit, the leading group tries to see that it is met.

Although the equipment in the neighborhood hospital is quite sparse, it seems adequate for the level of health work performed there. Simple laboratory tests and X-rays are available. The institution appears to function at a level not unlike that of many neighborhood health centers in the United States, one difference, of course, being the great use of traditional Chinese medical techniques. In addition, the coverage and intensity of the public-health work performed by the hospital appears to far exceed that of most such urban centers in the United States.

During the course of two hours one afternoon, Dr. Yang Yi-chin, of the Department of Internal Medicine, saw seventeen patients in a large room in which three other doctors were also seeing patients. The patient sat near Dr. Yang's desk while the history was taken. If a simple physical examination was needed such as inspection of the throat or auscultation of the heart or lungs, it was done with the patient sitting. If a more complete examination was needed, the patient was taken behind a screen to the single examining table shared by all four doctors.

Of the seventeen patients seen by Dr. Yang during one afternoon thirteen were female and four, including a thirteen-year-old, were male. Six had upper respiratory infections, five high blood pressure, and the remainder a variety of other illnesses amenable to ambulatory care. The following are examples of the patients Dr. Yang saw and the way they were handled:

A thirty-year-old policeman complained of a cold with headache and cough for two days. Dr. Yang inspected his throat and listened to his heart and lungs. The patient had no fever. Dr. Yang diagnosed an "upper respiratory infection" and gave the patient an antibiotic and cough medicine.

A heavy forty-eight-year-old woman complained of sweating, faintness, sleeplessness, and palpitations of the heart. The doctor took her blood pressure and listened to the patient's heart and found them both normal. He ordered a test for anemia, and the patient left to have it done in the hospital laboratory. She returned about thirty minutes later with the results of the test, which were normal. The doctor's impression was that she was having menopausal symptoms. He prescribed vitamin B_1, Librium, and another tranquilizer and told the patient to return in one week.

A vivacious woman of about thirty, who is a performer in the Peking Opera production of *Red Lantern*, has mild hypertension and came to the hospital to have her blood pressure measured. This was done, in both arms. It was normal, and no change in medication was made.

A forty-three-year-old woman, employed by the Department of Housing in the Fengsheng Neighborhood, complained of loss of appetite, feeling faint, sore throat, cough, difficulty in breathing, and sweating. Dr. Yang checked her blood pressure, her heart, her tongue, and her throat. His diagnosis was mild hypertension, and he prescribed drugs to lower her blood pressure, and vitamin B_1. The patient also wanted to see a doctor of traditional Chinese medicine and went to see him. Dr. Yang asked her to return in three days.

In short, with some differences in treatment patterns—for example, the use of antibiotics for what appeared to the observers to be a relatively mild viral upper respiratory infection and the use of traditional Chinese medicine—Dr. Yang's practice was similar to that of a physician in a neighborhood health center or in general practice in the United States.

There is little turnover of physicians at the hospital. Usually the patients see whatever doctor is available, but if a patient makes a special request, he can see a specific doctor. Salaries for the hospital doctors range from 46 to 155 yuan per month; traditional and Western-trained doctors have the same salary scale. Nurses begin at 40 yuan per month; the highest-paid nurse at the hospital in the fall of 1972 earned 69 yuan a month. Administrative personnel earn from 40 to 70 yuan a month.

Health care, perhaps better than any other single facet of Chinese society, vividly illustrates some of the principles that guide life in China today: a strong belief in mass involvement; recruitment of health workers from among those who live in the community to be served; short periods of training to minimize alienation from the community; a minimum of social distance between the helper and the helped; attempts to demystify as much of medicine as possible; decentralization; and motivating people through altruism rather than through prestige or material incentives (otherwise known as "fame and gain"). Medical care has been important to the Chinese government from the outset; it is perhaps the area in which the Chinese have had their most resounding success. Perhaps this success is due, at least to some degree, to the belief in and imaginative use of these principles.

NOTES

[1] Theodore H. White and Annalee Jacoby, *Thunder Out of China* (New York: William Sloane Associates, Inc., 1946), pp. 5–10.

[2] Rewi Alley, *Leaves from a Sandan Notebook* (Christchurch, New Zealand: The Caxton Press, 1950), p. 15.

[3] Han Suyin, "Reflections on Social Change," *Bulletin of the Atomic Scientists*, Vol. XXII, No. 6 (June, 1966), pp. 80–83.

[4] Mao Tse-tung, "On Practice," *Four Essays on Philosophy* (Peking: Foreign Languages Press, 1966), p. 8.

[5] Chen Wen-chieh and Ha Hsien-wen, "Medical and Health Work in New China," unpublished talk given by two Chinese physicians during a visit to Canada in November, 1971.

[6] Mao Tse-tung, "June 26 'Directive' (June 26, 1965)," *Red Medical Battle Bulletin and August 18 Battle Bulletin Commemorative Issue*, June 26, 1967, trans. in *Survey of China Mainland Press*, 198 supp. (1967), p. 30.

THE CHAI FAMILY

At Number 17 Da Chang lane in the Fengsheng Neighborhood Chai Chih-hsing, fifty-two years old, and his forty-eight-year-old wife, Wu Kuei-feng, live in a courtyard that they share with three other families. Comrade Chai has a lean angular face; he is wearing blue pants, a blue shirt, and leather sandals. His wife, a bit plump, her face smiling and welcoming, also wears blue pants, a blue short-sleeved blouse, and canvas shoes. In their gray-brick house trimmed around the windows and doors with red and green wood, Comrade Chai, his wife, and their son, Chai Tie-cheng, and his wife, Kuo Hsiu-hua, who live in the next courtyard at Number 19 Da Chang, talk about their lives.

The elder Comrade Chai begins, "I work in the women's hospital repairing medical equipment from eight in the morning until twelve noon and then from two in the afternoon until six. Before Liberation I also repaired machinery, but I could not get steady work. For the past twenty years I have been working at this hospital." Comrade Chai bikes to work twenty minutes away every day except Sunday, which is his day off.

His wife, Comrade Wu, does cleaning work in the same hospital, but whereas her husband bikes to work morning and evening, she goes by bus. "I just began working eleven years ago. The children were grown up. There was no need to stay at home any longer, and most of the women go to work. Before, women were not equal, and men looked down upon us; we were oppressed and could not work. Today it is different." Comrade Chai earns 80 yuan per month, and his wife earns 38. They have two other children, a daughter, twenty-two, who is a teacher in Heilungkiang province in northeast China and whom they see only once a year when she comes home to visit, and a son, twenty, who works in a steel factory in one of Peking's suburbs and lives in a dormitory near the factory. He comes home to visit every Sunday.

Out of their total income of 118 yuan per month, Comrade Chai and his wife pay a monthly rent of 4 yuan and 40 fen, just under 4 percent of their income. In addition, they pay 80 fen for electricity and water for their small two-room home. "We use our extra money to buy clothes, a bicycle, perhaps a watch," Comrade Chai said slowly. He continued, "And we save about forty to fifty yuan a month in the bank." When asked about the cost of food, Comrade Wu said that they spend about 20 yuan per person per month on food; they get lunch at the factory but have breakfast and dinner at home.

Comrade Wu said that her day off is Friday, but she added, "My free day is not fixed; every two weeks I have Sunday off with my husband." On their days off the couple do their chores around the house—clean their rooms, wash their clothes. They might go to a park nearby and occasionally will go sight-seeing, perhaps to the Great Wall.

Comrade Chai's son, Chai Tie-cheng, twenty-five, works in the First Steel Factory fifteen minutes away by bicycle but still in the West District of Peking. After he attended middle technical school for four years, he began working at the factory and has worked there now for five years. Kuo Hsiu-hua, his wife of six months, was dressed in pants and a blue plaid blouse. She has a young, delicate, tentative face and wears her hair in short pigtails. She said softly, "I have been working in a metal factory for four years. I went to primary school and then to secondary middle school for three years. I, too, go to work by bike; it takes me twenty minutes." When asked how the young couple met, both couples broke into laughter. The older Comrade Chai answered that his daughter-in-law's father worked at the same factory as his son and that he introduced them. They knew each other for two years before they married.

"When we decided to get married," Chai Tie-cheng recounted as his wife, upon the instructions of her father-in-law, got up to serve tea and apples, "we went to the Fengsheng Neighborhood Committee and told the special cadre in charge of marriage that we wished to be married. We went to Fengsheng because we planned to live here; we would have gone to the neighborhood committee for our marriage certificate wherever we planned to live. We were given a certificate which stated that we were now married. Afterward, our colleagues, relatives, and friends got together in our new home to sing songs and have a party." Upon questioning they said that they would like to have two children after a while and that they have no preference between boys and girls.

Young Chai and his wife together earn seventy-six yuan per month. They pay only two yuan per month for one room in the neighborhood and estimate that they spend approximately ten yuan per month for food. Nevertheless, they say that they are able to save between ten and twenty yuan per month. They have the same day off, Tuesday, and they usually spend it washing clothes, cleaning the courtyard, and sight-seeing. (The families who live together in the courtyard do not take turns maintaining the courtyard; they just work on it when they have time.)

Both couples were interested in life in the United States and asked specifically about workers' salaries and old-age pensions. There seemed to be a relaxed feeling, an easy give-and-take between the two couples, the two generations.

CHAPTER 5

WORK: We Are Determined to Make Greater Contributions

> Experts are pushed aside in favor of decision-making by "the masses"; new industries are established in rural areas; the educational system favors the disadvantaged....
>
> Maoists build ... to involve everyone in the development process, to pursue development without leaving a single person behind.
> —John G. Gurley, "Capitalist and
> Maoist Economic Development"

THE CENTRAL OFFICE of the production group of the Fengsheng Neighborhood is located in a small house inside a courtyard filled with green plants and bushes. Comrade Pan, the vice-chairman of the neighborhood's revolutionary committee, leads visitors through the courtyard to the front door of the house, where several smiling women wait proudly to show their work. White tablecloths meticulously embroidered with flowers, and babies' knitted dresses, hats, and booties in white, yellow, and pale blue decorated in contrasting pastel colors with flowers or animals, are spread out on long tables in the center of the room and along the walls. The production group was originally organized, according to one of the women workers, by the neighborhood committee to provide work for local housewives who "have children and cannot go out to work." The children's clothing and tablecloths are machine-made in a local factory and then sent over to the neighborhood for the embroidery, the

making of buttonholes, and the sewing on of buttons. The housewives, all of whom seem to be in their forties or fifties, are paid
directly per item by the factory.

A large red-brick building houses the Fengsheng Neighborhood Insulation Material Factory. The factory, established as
part of the Great Leap Forward in 1958, produces insulation
material for electrical machines. In a large conference room
with a television set in one corner but without a picture of Mao
Tse-tung on the walls (something that would have been unthink-
able just one year earlier) Chang Liang, the chairman of the
revolutionary committee, a tall man in his mid-thirties who, like
many other Chinese men, smokes his cigarettes down to his
fingertips, told about the history of the factory: "In the old
society housewives didn't work, but after Liberation women's
lives began to change. When this factory was started in nineteen
fifty-eight, all of the workers were housewives, but since the
Cultural Revolution we have a hundred and ninety workers—
thirty-four men and a hundred fifty-six women. Eighty-three
middle-school graduates have also come to work here as apprentices to learn their jobs from more experienced workers."
Comrade Chang pointed out that the apprentice system existed
before Liberation, too, but then apprentices earned hardly any
money. Today an apprentice earns sixteen yuan the first year
(really only a subsistence wage, but they are all young people,
still living at home, and therefore have minimal expenses),
eighteen yuan the second year, and the third year they earn a
regular worker's salary. To supplement their income, they are
given bus fare and medical care, haircuts, and admission to films
as well as a yearly clothing allowance of twenty-five yuan. These
apprentices are treated much the same as university students,
who receive a stipend of nineteen yuan per month in addition
to many free services. Regular workers at the insulation factory
earn between forty and sixty yuan per month, still a relatively
low salary by Chinese standards.

The factory is run by a five-member revolutionary committee, four of whom are women. The revolutionary committee was established March 7, 1968, as a direct result of the struggles of the Cultural Revolution. Prior to that time Chang Liang, the current chairman of the committee, was the director. In 1968 the workers first selected the five members of the committee, and the committee subsequently chose the chairman and two vice-chairmen. The entire structure then had to be approved by the neighborhood committee. It happens, not infrequently, that those who were directors or managers or chairmen before the Cultural Revolution have once again been placed in leading positions, often following a period of criticism, self-criticism, and sometimes even some time at a May 7 school in the country-side where through physical labor and political study they can "remold their thinking." But now these people in leadership roles are often surrounded by a committee to aid in the administration or at least to watch over the shoulder of the administrator. Comrade Chang verified this observation by commenting that in most factories the former manager had been elected chairman of the revolutionary committee, and the person in charge of production had been named the new vice-chairman. It is, of course, very difficult to evaluate whether this reinstatement has occurred because these were competent, knowledgeable people from the start and should still be tapped for their expertise and administrative ability, albeit with a more representative, democratic structure to work within, or whether during the Cultural Revolution some segments of the established bureaucracy managed to hold firm to their positions and, to some extent, prevent the recruitment of new leadership. It would seem that both explanations are at least in part valid, but in talking with people in leadership positions in schools, factories, and neighborhoods, one's overwhelming impression is of people with enormous competence and ability. And in spite of revolutionary zeal, a desire to shake up the bureaucracy, a wish to eliminate elitism wherever possible and to ensure popular participation, China's leaders apparently do not wish to, and indeed cannot afford to, lose the talents of such able administrators.

To return to the structure of the revolutionary committee of the Fengsheng Insulation Material Factory, Comrade Chang continued, "Not all of the members of the committee are cadres; some are simply representatives of the masses. For example, a person who works in the dining room is on the committee and is an ordinary worker, not a cadre. Cadres are, however, usually in charge of the main work, and they, together with the workers, decide on policy matters." In response to questions about the role of the Communist party, Comrade Chang said that 7 to 8 percent of the workers are members of the party and that he himself is secretary of the local Communist party group within the factory. "The role of the Communist party," he elaborated, "is to lead the people through democratic discussion." The workers are organized into study groups of ten to twenty people and spend six hours a week, after working hours, studying and discussing important political and work-related issues.

The tasks of the revolutionary committee are threefold (in the order Comrade Chang named them): (1) "to carry out the policies of the Communist party and Chairman Mao's revolutionary line," (2) "to organize the workers to study Marxism–Leninism–Mao Tse-tung Thought," and (3) "to organize production and to raise the level of production and of technical quality."

Located in a series of courtyards in the West District of Peking, the First Transistor Equipment Factory is somewhat larger, employing 360 workers. It, too, was begun as a neighborhood factory during the Great Leap Forward of 1958. According to the chairman of the revolutionary committee, Liu Hsin-chuan, this factory now manufactures diffusion furnaces for transistor production. China had to import such equipment at a cost of 25,000 yuan per furnace prior to 1965. According to Comrade Liu, "In nineteen sixty-five Tsinghua University began research on methods for the manufacture of transistors and needed a factory to test the methods; they chose this factory. Originally only housewives who did repairing work by hand worked here.

"When we were chosen to be the testing factory for Tsinghua University, we had four main difficulties: We only had a hundred ninety square meters of working space; we had very simple equipment; the hundred and ten workers who worked here had a low technical level (only one had finished secondary middle school); and we had insufficient funds. We had a long discussion under the leadership of the party branch and studied Chairman Mao's teachings about hard work and self-reliance.

"The workers were determined to create conditions to test the new equipment. First they built an additional workshop of twenty square meters, and then they selected a small group of ten workers to go to Tsinghua University to learn how to build the machines. This group was made up of one worker with secondary-middle-school education, an accountant, and eight housewives.

"But the workers had problems learning at Tsinghua. They were not used to studying; they were used to doing physical labor, and when they were asked to read blueprints for the machinery, they got headaches. They were given pills for their headaches, and the students and the teachers of the university helped them with their work. In two months they had mastered the needed skills and returned to this factory to teach the other workers and to begin production. After seven months we began to have some success." That was in 1966. Today the factory produces diffusion furnaces for more than twenty provinces and proudly reported that three of their products were exhibited in a recent Canton trade fair. The factory workers still do most of their work by hand. Nevertheless, at a cost that ranges from 6,500 to 8,500 yuan per furnace, they produce the machinery at one third of the cost of importing it. The factory's facilities have gradually been improved except for one shop that has been left as it was when the factory began in 1958 to remind the workers of former times.

The factory personnel are divided into groups, some of which test components made by other groups. Most of the workers are simultaneously working and studying in order to increase their knowledge of transistor production. For example, Wang Chin-tsai is a housewife and mother of three children who lives near the factory. She has been working here for ten years, and although she had only two years of primary-school education, she was one of the original workers who went to Tsinghua University for special training. She was also one of the workers who developed headaches when she needed to read blueprints. According to Comrade Wang, "After several years of practice I have mastered some of the techniques but still have a lack of knowledge of theory and will continue to study."

The factory provides a small nursery and kindergarten for the children of the workers and also provides medical care for the workers. A young woman wearing a yellow and gray plaid shirt and pigtails and looking ten years younger than her thirty-one years is one of the two worker-doctors at the factory. She has been interested in medical work since she was a child, she explained, and when the doctor from the district hospital came to the factory to recruit worker-doctors, she expressed her interest. The factory's revolutionary committee subsequently chose her to be a medical worker. She then spent three months part-time in early 1970 in a training course given in the factory by a doctor from a local hospital. Later she spent two months in the neighborhood hospital learning acupuncture and the technique of giving injections. Worker-doctors, like their rural counterparts, the barefoot doctors, spend part of their time doing their regular jobs in the factory and part of their time doing medical work. And like the neighborhood medical workers, they treat only "minor illnesses"—bronchitis, diarrhea, headaches, fever, colds.

Family planning receives special attention within the factory; it is under the auspices of a special subcommittee of the revolutionary committee and the local party branch. The worker-doctor dispenses birth-control methods free and keeps records that include the name of the worker, her age, the number of children she already has, the number she would like to have, the spacing she would prefer, and the birth-control method that she is using. The worker-doctors, both women, work only with female workers, apparently due to the traditional Chinese reluctance to cross sex lines in dealing with sexual matters. The wives of male workers are generally working in other factories, and their birth-control needs are met in their own places of work.

Abortion is available to those women whose birth-control methods fail. The usual procedure is for the worker to discuss her needs for an abortion first with the worker-doctor and then be referred to the district hospital or the neighborhood hospital where the abortion is done. The worker is entitled to ten to fifteen days' leave with pay after an abortion. The worker-doctors feel that the optimal number of children is two and that many women stop at that number, "even if they have only two girls or two boys."

The Peking Printing and Dyeing Mill in Peking's northeast district of Chao yang, a large factory employing some 2,200 workers, was also established in 1958. According to the leading member, Chang Chun-pao, a man in his forties, his black hair mixed with gray and his manner serious and professional, the main task of the factory is to print and dye cotton cloth. The process begins at the design shop where artists create the designs that will be printed on the fabric and is continued with the carving of the designs onto rollers; the rollers are then etched and brought to the shop in which the fabric is printed. Comrade Chang was critical of the work of the factory before the Cultural Revolution: "Before the Cultural Revolution our equipment was not adequate, and we did not fulfill the needs for cloth. We only produced forty-five million meters. During the Cultural Revolution workers studied ways of increasing production, and by nineteen seventy we were producing a hundred and two million meters of cloth. In every shop we organized groups of older, more experienced workers and cadres to think about ways of improving quality. We now have new equipment, some of which is made in China and some imported. The equipment is important in raising production, but the workers are more important."

To provide for the health needs of the workers, the Printing and Dyeing Mill has quite an elaborate health facility including the services of six Western-trained doctors, nine nurses, one pharmacist, and twenty-eight worker-doctors. Since 42 percent of the workers in the Printing and Dyeing Mill are women, women's needs are given special attention by the medical personnel at the factory. The yearly checkups of female workers include a breast examination and vaginal and cervical smears. Prenatal care is also given at the factory: Women are seen once a month until the seventh month of pregnancy, after which they are seen once every two weeks; during the last month they are examined once a week. During these checkups their blood pressure is taken, the position of the baby checked, and urinalysis done. When the woman is in her seventh month of pregnancy, she is given lighter work, and after delivery she has the traditional fifty-six-day maternity leave.

At the end of her paid maternity leave the mother receives a postpartum physical exam before she goes back to work. She is then free to bring her baby to the factory nursing room and may leave her work twice during the day, at nine in the morning and at one in the afternoon, to nurse her baby. Nursery teachers are also given special medical attention, as are the children who receive their immunizations there.

Women's health needs are further met by a ten-day paid sick leave after an abortion that has been performed before the end of two months of pregnancy and a fourteen-day paid leave when the abortion has been performed after two months of pregnancy. As in other Chinese settings abortion seemed to be available without stigma to married women but is seen not as a primary birth-control measure but rather as a method to be used when there has been a failure of other methods.

The factory has a series of medical consultation rooms: a small surgical department for minor wounds, a laboratory and injection room, an acupuncture department, a pharmacy, and a simple ward where a worker can stay overnight because of illness or for diagnostic reasons. The factory also provides dormitories for single and married workers and a dining hall in which workers can take their meals; some of the workers even grow vegetables near the factory for use in the kitchen.

Pay differentials within the factory are perhaps greater than one might expect. The lowest pay for a beginning worker is 35 yuan per month, according to Comrade Chang, and the highest pay for the most experienced worker is 240 yuan per month. The salary for a fully trained doctor starts at 46 yuan per month, rises to 56 yuan per month the second year, and can rise as high as 170 yuan per month, 70 yuan less than an experienced worker earns. Middle medical doctors and nurses begin at a lower salary, 32 yuan per month for the first year, 37 yuan the second year. Nurses' salaries rise only to 80 yuan per month, less than one half of the salary of the highest-paid doctor and only one third of the salary of the highest-paid worker. A substantial part of the factory budget, 11 percent, is used for medical and welfare funds; the use of these funds is determined by the twenty-one-member revolutionary committee, which is made up of representatives of workers from each shop and, in spite of the emphasis on medical work at the factory, does not include any doctors. Absence due to illness for one or more days in the course of any given month is only about 5.5 percent of the factory's workers; this amounts to ten to twenty workers—less than 1 percent of the work force—absent on an average day, an extremely low rate of absenteeism.

The factory is thus not simply a place of work; it is rather an extension of one's home. In China one's work is not kept separate or compartmentalized from one's home or private life. To the contrary, there has been the ongoing attempt to integrate living and working, and the provision of services such as medical care and day care at the place of work aids in this integration.

This can best be illustrated, perhaps, by the following account of a divorce trial. It took place in Police Traffic Substation 6 in the West District of Peking, where the husband works as a traffic policeman. The wife works for the district housing administration department. It is particularly noteworthy that representatives of both the husband's work unit and the wife's work unit, in addition to friends, are present and participating in the trial. As is usual in divorce cases, every effort was made to reconcile the husband and wife, first through the neighborhood or factory committee and then, only if that fails, through the court.

Present at this divorce case are the wife, who is the plaintiff, the husband, who is the defendant, representatives of the revolutionary committee, representatives of both the husband's and the wife's work units, the chief judge, a second judge, an assistant judge, and several comrades or friends.

Chief Judge: Our procedure is for the parties to the case and the masses to participate and make proposals, using criticism and self-criticism. Tell us your age and nationality.

Wife: 33 years old; Han; middle peasant family from Hopei Province; middle school education.

Chief Judge: Salary?

Wife: 41 yen per month.

Husband: 39; Han; Peking middle peasant; junior middle school.

Chief Judge: Salary?

Husband: 70 yen per month.

Chief Judge: What are your reasons for seeking a divorce?

Wife: We got acquainted through introduction by friends. Married in 1961; daughter born 1962. Had usual feelings of newly-married couple. Then I got maternal disease of irregular menses and had to stay home from work for two months. I still suffer from this illness. This led to conflicts in our sex life. At first we forgave each other, but as time passed, this was no longer possible. I myself was at fault and was often unhappy, although my husband was often quite understanding. He said that I should not become pregnant again because of this disease. Thereafter our sex life was not good. So I said this was not good for family life, and my grandmother proposed that I get a divorce and I thought this was reasonable. She told my husband that he could not sacrifice his spiritual life because I was sick. She told him that he was still in good condition and must consider future generations. For myself, I was still reluctant to get divorced, but thought I could take care of our child. Often I was very sorry, but often too sick to get up. Sometimes my husband could not suppress his sexual desires. Our Constitution says if marriage is not feasible, the couple can be separated for the sake of work and daily life.

Husband: Our problem is of long standing. She says her disease is the main problem, and she is really sick, but I do not think it is as serious as she says. The main thing is her mental feeling; the spiritual burden on her is very heavy. I think the problem can be solved, but now, since she says we should be separated, I cannot but agree.

Chief Judge: How long did you know each other before marriage?

Husband: About two years. We fell in love in May, 1959. I worked in this office; she lived in the dormitory of the office building and worked on the construction team there. Later we met through an official introduction.

Chief Judge: Tell us how you felt about each other before marriage and right afterward?

Wife: Those were the best times, but just so-so; not very bad or good. At times I thought he was quite good in some respects. Before the birth of our child, sex relations were good.

Representative of Husband's Work Unit: Feelings appear quite good before then.

Chief Judge: Describe conflicts and basic relations.

Husband: Generally good. Busy with work. I had heavy tasks, had to travel; she handled family affairs. Until she suggested in 1968 that I suppress my sex desires. Then there was trouble. Before 1968 no big conflicts. Let her tell about conflicts.

Assistant Judge: Has your husband stated all the main reasons?

Wife: Yes.

Chief Judge: [reviewing husband's story] Did the misunderstandings change in character? Did they become deeper? Help us analyze the case. Your comrades know about you, but your expressions will help us to handle the contradictions according to Chairman Mao's teaching and laws. For example, when did the contradictions become very sharp?

Wife: Sharpened after 1968. My disease was worse and I felt very bored. Quarrels could not be avoided, also misunderstandings. I was sick and he could not understand me very well.

Chief Judge: First, your sickness; second, married life no good; third, misunderstandings. Also the wife felt the husband did not show enough consideration. Right?

Husband: In addition, we now have no affection; the sentiment has been broken. This has affected our work, confused our minds. After many years, I agreed to separation.

Chief Judge: How old is your child now?

Husband: Ten.

Chief Judge: Have you ever talked to her about separating?

Wife: No.

Husband: No, but she knows that we quarrel.

Chief Judge: We must consider whether the situation is serious enough to warrant separation. Describe the worst quarrel.

Wife: You say.

Husband: She was to handle family affairs, but she spent her own salary and then often came to my office to find me. Often she went to the responsible leadership for help. She could not work well, due to her illness. We never cursed each other or fought. We went to comrades and finally to court for help.

Chief Judge: Your husband says you did not pay attention to family affairs; made a disturbance in his work unit, and aroused bad feelings toward him.

Wife: Basically true.

Chief Judge: Apart from buying something for your child, you spent your own salary and made trouble. Yes?

Wife: Yes.

Chief Judge: You did not show consideration for your wife, though she had done enough as a revolutionary partner? According to article 8 of the Marriage Law, spouses are to love, help and raise children together. When there are shortcomings, they are to be solved through criticism and self-criticism.

Husband: Generally I was all right about carrying out my obligations. After she proposed separation, my feelings were hurt; then sometimes I showed insufficient consideration.

Chief Judge: What about plans for your child?

Wife: Since kindergarten at age 4, she has been living with my husband's mother in the countryside because we are working here. I pay half her expenses for clothing and so forth.

Chief Judge: Why not tell [the] child?

Wife: Too young; it might affect her mentally and make her unhappy. I will tell her when she is older.

Chief Judge: [to Representatives of Work Units] You know details better than we do. Leading comrades, please give us your description of the situation and your ideas.

Representative of Wife's Work Unit: We first learned of the troubles in 1969 when the wife brought bedding to sleep in our station. We asked her why. She was too shy to tell the details because I am a man, so I asked a woman comrade to talk with her and get details. We gave help, education for unity. Then she returned home, but there were frequent disputes and we tried to work with them. The situation was better, then worse, etc. As to her demand for separation, we think more work should be done before this is accepted, but her demand was urgent, so we signed approval.

Representative of Wife's Work Unit: I talked with the wife in 1969 when she came with bedding and child. I expressed my concern for the child and her view of her parents. I said there should be more self-criticism by husband and wife to see strong points of each. I pointed out her workplace was too far from the child's school and that she would arouse her husband's suspicions if she stayed at the workplace; that is not a correct way to handle conflicts.

Representative of Work Unit: [also from wife's unit voiced similar views]

Wife: The grandmother is reluctant to have the child leave her.

Comrade: How can you as parents leave your own child if the grandmother cannot?

Assistant Judge: [after reviewing everyone's list of the problems] If the husband shows more consideration during menses, maybe this will help solve the problems. Contradictions about sex life are not big contradictions. Perhaps a family meeting with the grandparents would help. There are no fundamental contradictions.

Representative of Husband's Work Unit: I have a good understanding of the husband, but don't know the wife well. My opinion now is that they have a good sentimental basis for marriage from their early years. The main contradiction is in sex life. Revolutionary comrades should keep each other, though they cannot agree on all matters. Both are responsible for situation. Why did the husband finally agree to divorce?

Very painful for him. His wife came here to see the leadership and sometimes she exaggerated her husband's misdeeds. This affected her husband's colleagues and embarrassed him. That's why he agreed to separation. The wife should try harder to cure her illness and he should show more understanding. Divorce is bad for the mind of a child. How can you as parents live apart from your own child? This must influence her feelings. Try to solve contradictions through criticism and self-criticism.

Husband's Friend: The contradiction can be solved. She can try more for a cure and he should try to understand. [While she reviews problems, husband's left leg and foot continuously jerk up and down.] And what happens to the child if you remarry? [Leader of husband's unit repeats previous speakers.]

Chief Judge: Both parties have suffered spiritually. Under article 17 of the Marriage Law, if both sides agree to a divorce, the court will approve. You should consider this again very seriously. Are you really at a stage where you should be separated? According to Chairman Mao, there are no fundamental contradictions within the working class. I see none between you. The basis for your marriage is good. Self-criticism can find defects and make it possible to continue the marriage. As to the wife's disease, medical facilities in our country can cure many now, and they are getting better. Do you think after hearing your comrades you can make more self-criticism and reconcile? [to wife] You want a divorce, but haven't told your child. This shows a contradiction in you, that you are still uncertain. [As Chief Judge continues, husband holds his forehead.]

Wife: You are earnest and frank. I am touched and grateful. But there is an acute struggle in my mind. If we reconcile and contradictions arise again, how will we resolve them? [Husband shows pained expression.] I must insist on my demand. This will save trouble for the leadership.

Chief Judge: Your mind is entangled with contradictions. Self-criticism will solve problems if you reconcile. Do you think all the fault is with your husband? If you reconcile and new problems arise, you can put forward certain demands on your husband. Have you really shown enough effort?

Comrade: You may repent later if you separate now. Better reconcile—better for work and politically.

Chief Judge: What do you say? I have misgivings about a separation. You ought to be reconciled, but I see you did not criticize yourself enough or make enough demands on your husband. In the future, make more demands on yourself and show more responsibility in the family. And I say to grandparents and husband: have a family meeting. Discuss the practical problems: the wife told exaggerated stories about the husband at his work unit. He lost face and it was not good for his work. And she is afraid of future complications.

Assistant Judge: Don't be afraid of contradictions. You will get help if they arise in the future. New unity can be reached and comrades will help.

Husband's Friend: Don't be afraid of future or about his attitude in future. He is a cadre with responsibilities.

Chief Judge: My final opinion is that this contradiction cannot be solved by divorce.

OTHERS SPEAK, MAINLY TO WIFE.

Chief Judge: Tell us your final decision. [to husband] If you agree, we must grant separation. [more comments to wife]

Woman Comrade: [to wife] Have faith in comrades as to future help.

Woman Assistant Judge: The wife wants her husband to express his feelings.

Chief Judge: [irritated] He already has. Have faith in comrades.

Assistant Judge: Your husband cannot be blamed for everything. In some respects your husband is quite good. He should improve.

Comrade: Do not fear your husband will make some reprisal against you. We know his political consciousness and integrity.

Comrade: Your husband treated you quite well despite your

hot temper. Your minds are now open to each other; life will be happier.

Chief Judge: Let's hear first from the wife.

Wife: You have been patient and given good advice. I would like to be reconciled. I will make more strict demands for help and will take more family responsibility. I withdraw my request for separation.

Husband: For years I did not agree to divorce until I felt I must. Since she now agrees not to separate, I agree. All details and future plans cannot be solved here, but the basis for the future is certain now.

Chief Judge: Look to your comrades and, if necessary, to court for help. Rest for a while. Wait in another room while we study the situation.

RECESS.

IN ABSENCE OF PARTIES AND WITNESSES, JUDGES CONFER.

Chief Judge: There is a very acute struggle in her mind.

[Discussion among judges. Agree to reconciliation; welcome it; must work on the next stage in the relationship, including the grandmother.]

PARTIES RETURN.

Chief Judge: We agree to your present view, that there is insufficient reason to separate and you now agree to reconcile. We have heard the wife's misgivings, and you must arrange for future meetings between yourselves, with your families, and within your work units. [to wife] Will you sign the minutes of the court?

WIFE SIGNS.

HUSBAND SIGNS.

Chief Judge: If you would like to read the minutes, you can come to court to read them and see if there are any mistakes.

HEARING CONCLUDED.[1]

Sian

The printing and binding factory at Number 12 Ching Nian Lu again illustrates the organizing and functioning of small satellite factories. In a reception room in which copies of *Renmin Ribao* (People's Daily) are hanging on the walls, visitors and worker representatives crowd around the table drinking tea as the director, Tsui Ching-yun, the mother of four children, tells the history of the factory: "This factory was set up in nineteen sixty-six at the beginning of the Cultural Revolution. There was no working shop then nor any equipment; the women just worked under a roof. According to Chairman Mao, housewives want to work just the same as the men, for they have two hands, too, and don't want to live idly. The women themselves went to the residents' committee and requested work. The residents' committee found a large printing factory nearby which needed to have work done, and fifteen went to the factory for one month full-time to learn the work while the other ten remained here and prepared space and a few simple tools. Then the four or five came back and trained the others. They all worked together under the roof folding paper, cutting covers, and binding simple books with a plastic cover."

Comrade Tsui continued: "Back in nineteen sixty-six the housewives earned only seven yuan per month, as they could only earn what their production was worth. As they produced more, they earned more. Now the housewives earn thirty-five yuan per month. Two men from outside of the area also work in the factory; both of them have greater technical skill than the women. One of them earns sixty-five yuan a month and the other forty-five."

The factory is completely self-sufficient; it pays the workers out of its earnings and uses any profit to enlarge the factory. The factory even provides a form of health insurance for its workers—each worker pays three yuan per year and then receives free medical care at the Ching Nian Lu Health Station. The factory also handles some welfare problems; if a worker becomes ill for a long period of time, she will receive her full

salary for six months, but when the six months is over, she will
then receive no further salary. Furthermore, if a worker or her
family has financial difficulties, they can get help from this
factory. Recently one worker had financial problems because
her husband was sick for a long period of time. All of the workers met together and decided "by open discussion" to give the
worker fifteen yuan. This decision was then approved by the
leading group. Comrade Tsui commented, however, that this
situation was quite unusual.

In dark crowded rooms off of the courtyard the workers fold
paper to make ledgers, fold envelopes for a large factory, and
make small envelopes in which medicine can be dispensed. They
sit grouped by twos and threes talking quietly, a teacup on each
worker's table. The two highly skilled men work at each end of
the large room, one operating a paper cutter, the other printing
the medical envelopes. The workers arrive at 7:30 in the morning and leave for lunch at 11:30. In the afternoon they return
at 1:30 and go home at 5:30. Because the larger factory that
farms the work out to them has its holiday on Monday, workers
in the Ching Nian Lu Printing and Binding Factory also have
their holiday on Monday.

In an adjoining courtyard still at Number 12 is the Ching
Nian Lu Refining Factory. Fifteen workers—fourteen housewives and one man—extract metals from waste water. In one
section they extract gold, which they then give to the bank. In
another alcove they are refining silver from developing fluid.
With huge aprons, goggles, head masks, and long heavy gloves
they work over a kiln extracting the silver.

During the day the workers have a ten-minute tea break
morning and afternoon, and on Tuesdays and Fridays they
remain late, from six to eight o'clock in the evening, to participate in their study groups. "On Tuesdays we study our professional technique, learn about model workers, and think how

to increase production," the workers said. "On Fridays we read the newspapers, read Mao Tse-tung, and study politics. We are determined to make greater contributions."

Shanghai

Two hundred and fifty women from the Kung Chiang New Village are making tiny light bulbs for flashlights in a local neighborhood factory. It is painstaking work, so taxing on the eyes of the workers that they are entitled to a ten-minute break every two hours. Like the printing and binding factory in Sian, this factory was organized in 1966, and all work is on consignment from a larger factory.

According to the responsible member of the factory, Hsiao Tsai-chu, "Every woman in Kung Chiang under the age of fifty works; there is not a single one who doesn't. But after the age of fifty the women stay at home to look after their grandchildren and do embroidery and knitting for the neighborhood."

Comrade Hsiao went on to say that the average worker earns thirty yuan per month. When this relatively low wage was commented on, she pointed out that all of the housewives (for some reason women who work in neighborhood factories in China are referred to as "housewives" rather than as "workers") have husbands working in larger factories and therefore presumably do not need to earn as much money as they would otherwise. She went on, "They are all happy that they can work together, that they are liberated from the house; they work not only for economic reasons but to contribute to socialist construction."

There is a clear conflict between the decentralization and self-reliance as practiced by the urban neighborhoods in their administration of local factories, the consequently low wage scale within these factories, and the liberation of women. It can be reasonably claimed that these housewives are being exploited by doing menial, relatively unskilled labor and being paid a low wage for it. The Chinese, however, compare the present with the past and see progress. Formerly women were bound to their families and their courtyards; today they are not. In addition, liberation is seen not only in terms of women performing skilled rather than unskilled labor or the amount of income earned but also in terms of a commitment on the part of women to working for the public good rather than simply being concerned with private matters involving the family.

Furthermore, the work done in small local factories is clearly only possible in a semi-industrialized society in which human labor is more economical than machinery. Under these circumstances workers with minimal skills can be trained to do a specific job and can therefore participate in both the economic process and the economic decision-making process.

These small satellite factories represent many facets of Chinese economic philosophy: the Chinese commitment to full employment, the belief in decentralization and in involving as many people as possible in decision-making, and the belief in self-reliance, or *tzu-li keng-sheng*. It is because of the deep commitment to these principles that the workers at the Ching Nian Lu Printing and Binding Factory could earn only seven yuan a month when the factory was first established and then gradually increased their wages as their profits increased. A subsidy from the city of Sian or the Lian Hu district would have undermined *tzu-li keng-sheng*, local decision-making, improvement through one's own hard work.

John G. Gurley, the American economist, points out that rather than building on "the best," as capitalism supposedly does, Maoist economics builds on the so-called worst in order to involve the greatest number of people:

Experts are pushed aside in favor of decision-making by "the masses"; new industries are established in rural areas; the educational system favors the disadvantaged; expertise (and hence work proficiency in a narrow sense) is discouraged; new products are domestically produced rather than being imported "more efficiently"; the growth of cities as centers of industrial and cultural life is discouraged; steel, for a time, is made by "everyone" instead of by only the much more efficient steel industry.

Maoists build on the worst not, of course, because they take great delight in lowering economic efficiency, but rather to involve everyone in the development process, to pursue development without leaving a single person behind . . . efficiency is being sacrificed to some extent for equity.[2]

But as Gurley goes on to say, Maoists believe that these economic policies will prove more effective in the long run by bringing everyone along, by eliminating the basis for a class without hope, a segment of the population without a stake in society. These policies, furthermore, are pursued with greater or less fervor depending, at least partially, on the political climate. During the Great Leap Forward and again during the Great Proletarian Cultural Revolution when the swing toward mass participation and away from experts and elitism was most intense, the policy of building on "the worst" seemed most prevalent. By 1972 the pendulum had begun to swing to some extent in the other direction.

NOTES

[1] Reprinted from Doris Brin Walker, "People's Court in China: Trial of a Divorce Case," *The National Lawyers Guild Practitioner*, Vol. XXX, Nos. 2–3 (Spring–Summer, 1973), pp. 45–53.

[2] John G. Gurley, "Capitalist and Maoist Economic Development," in Edward Friedman and Mark Selden, eds., *America's Asia: Dissenting Essays on Asian-American Relations* (New York: Vintage Books, 1971), p. 339.

THE WANG FAMILY

Wang Shu-mei, a lively, attractive woman of thirty-six whose ready smile crinkles up her eyes, lives at Number 21 Ching Nian Lu in Sian. She, her mother, and her three children—two boys, sixteen and ten, and a girl of twelve—live three courtyards in from the road in a small gray-brick attached house with a slanted gray-tile roof. Four other families live in the courtyard with Comrade Wang; twelve families, approximately fifty people, live in the three courtyards of Number 21 Ching Nian Lu.

Dressed in a blue and white print blouse, taupe pants, and a brown corduroy jacket, her hair shaped so that it has a slight wave (unlike most Chinese women, whose hair is clipped bluntly), Comrade Wang nervously twists her hands as she talks with her Western visitors. "We originally came from Tientsin, where my husband and I were married seventeen years ago. We have lived in Sian since our marriage but have only lived on this street for three years. We moved here to be nearer to my work; now it only takes me five minutes to get there by bicycle." Comrade Wang works in a political group at a film-publishing house. She has been a cadre for eight years; before that she worked directly in the production of films. Her husband, a member of the People's Liberation Army, has been stationed in Peking since 1958. He spends one month a year in Sian with his family, and she visits him in Peking once or twice a year. He will soon be transferred back to Sian, she hopes, perhaps this year. Comrade Wang's mother and father live in different cities also. Her mother lives with her, but her father lives with her brother and his family in Paoting, Hopei province.

Comrade Wang and her family use each of their three rooms as a bedroom as well as a place to eat, to study, and simply to relax. Comrade Wang and her daughter sleep in the room farthest from the front door, a room with a stone floor and white stucco walls, a large bed, a chest of drawers made out of what looks to be a reddish-brown mahogany, two tables, and several stools. On the wall are snapshots of the family, a mirror, and a calendar; on one of the tables, a radio and a clock. A sewing machine sits in the corner of the room, and the drawers of both the tables and the chest are locked with small blue locks.

Comrade Wang's mother looks startlingly like her daughter. Her serious, deeply lined face can break out into a broad smile with little provocation; she wears her gray hair pulled back into a bun in the back of her head, and her gray Mao jacket nearly matches her hair. She sleeps in the middle room with the younger son. The older boy sleeps alone in the third and smallest room, the one into which the front door opens. To get to Comrade Wang's room, one must walk through the other two.

Comrade Wang works in the mornings until noon, when she and the three children all come home for lunch, which has been prepared by the grandmother. After lunch and a nap they return to work and to school at two o'clock. Comrade Wang does not return home again until six in the evening, when her mother is preparing dinner.

Every family has their own very simple cooking facilities in a semi-protected alcove beside the house. In the summer they usually cook outside. Toilet facilities, cement slabs over a hole in the ground, are communal for the courtyard; the feces, or "night soil" as it is known in China, is collected by a municipal-level agency two or three times a week and transported to the countryside to be used as fertilizer. The families have a spigot in the courtyard with running water, which must be heated if they need hot water.

Comrade Wang's younger children attend primary school at Number 31 Ching Nian Lu. Her daughter, in her last year of primary school, is very skilled at table tennis. She is somewhat unusual in that she plays Ping-Pong with her left hand as well as her right, but is even better with her left. With left-handed players in China quite rare, her Ping-Pong is being carefully cultivated at a workers' club in the west suburb of Sian, where she spends Monday, Tuesday, Thursday, Friday, and Saturday afternoons improving her skills. Since she was chosen by the municipality to receive this special training, she is transported to the club and home again by city bus. Twice a week she returns to school in the evening for an hour and a half so that a teacher can help her catch up on her studies. It is evidently not so unusual for students from this primary school to be specifically selected for their Ping-Pong ability. The school's Ping-Pong team has held the district championship for several years, and the school makes a special effort to train its students in "physical culture."

Comrade Wang's sons both like to paint, and they belong to a painting group that meets after school and on Saturday mornings. On Sunday, Comrade Wang's day off from work, they all like to go to the park together, but the grandmother stays home to do the cooking.

Comrade Wang and her husband together earn 150 yuan per month. After they pay 1.4 yuan per month for rent, 40 or 50 fen per month for electricity and water, 30 yuan per month for food, and perhaps 200 yuan per year for clothing, Comrade Wang is still able to save 80 yuan per month in the savings bank nearby, where her money earns 4 percent interest per year.

CHAPTER 6

EDUCATION: Studying for the Revolution

> The sun is red;
> The sun is bright;
> The sun shines all over
> Like a sunflower. . . .
> The sun is the Communist party;
> The sun is Chairman Mao!
> —Sung by two-and-a-half-year-olds,
> Ta Cheng Nursery, Peking

A GROUP of thirty five-year-olds sit on small chairs in a semi-circle on the stone floor of the Ta Cheng Kindergarten under a picture of Chairman Mao and sing "All Sing the East Is Red." One small girl in a peach-colored dress with a fuchsia bow and green socks dances while four others, accompanied by their teacher at the organ, sing "Put Chairman Mao's Badge on Your Chest to Show Your Love for Chairman Mao." Their next song is "I Am a Small Member of the People's Commune," one girl leading, four others following, all dancing, skipping, and singing.

In another room with a stone floor and carved dark wood around the windows thirty-one six-year-olds sit in a semicircle singing folk songs of national minority groups, their young teacher, wearing long pigtails and a bright pink blouse, accompanying them at the organ.

A group of two-and-a-half-year-olds sit out in the courtyard on a warm sunny autumn day, eating their noodles out of small bowls. When they have finished lunch, they sing, "The sun is red; the sun is bright; the sun shines all over like a sunflower.

. . . The sun is the Communist party; the sun is Chairman Mao!"

Two hundred and thirty children attend the Ta Cheng Nursery and Kindergarten in the Fengsheng Neighborhood, and thirty-one teachers, including Chiu Shih-lan, the vice-chairman of the revolutionary committee, care for them. According to Comrade Chiu, "This kindergarten was set up by four housewives in nineteen fifty-five. They started with forty children in three rooms, but in nineteen fifty-eight many housewives started to work and needed to send their children to kindergarten. The four original housewives had to work hard to educate the children and to enable other housewives to work.

"From nineteen fifty-eight on, the kindergarten grew until today we have forty-four teachers and staff members and two hundred and thirty children. The children range in age from fifty-six days, the end of the Chinese woman's paid maternity leave, to seven years. They are divided according to ages into eight classes. Most children arrive at seven thirty in the morning and leave at six in the evening, but forty children stay overnight during the week, go home on Saturday evening, and return on Monday morning."

In the nursery thirteen teachers care for sixty-seven children under the age of three. Growing up is a collective affair; toilet training is begun at ten months with all the babies sitting side by side on small white enamel potties after meals and then taking naps two to a crib. Meals are, of course, taken in large groups. The children receive three meals a day and snacks. As the children grow older, math, language, arts and crafts, music, and physical exercise are added to their activities; the younger group has one period of study a day, and the middle and older groups have two.

In describing the goals of the Ta Cheng Nursery and Kindergarten, Comrade Chiu stated emphatically, "We want to teach the children to love their leader, to love their motherland, to love labor, the people, and the collective. We teach them through stories and pictures, through singing revolutionary songs, through painting, and even through exercise. Chairman Mao has taught that we must participate in physical culture to improve the health of the people, and every morning we have one period of exercise."

The health of the children is of great importance to the staff of Ta Cheng. Before the children may enter school, they must be examined in the Fengsheng Neighborhood Hospital—two examinations per year if they are under eighteen months and one if they are older. A doctor from the neighborhood hospital comes to the kindergarten to give the physical exams and to give the children their immunizations.

The kindergarten is mainly supported by the fees that the parents pay or, if necessary, by supplementary funds from the Fengsheng Neighborhood Committee. The parents whose children come only during the day pay twelve yuan per month per child—six yuan for food and six yuan for tuition. Those whose children remain overnight during the week pay sixteen yuan per month. If the mother is a factory worker, the factory will pay half of the six yuan that covers educational expenses; the parents are expected to pay the entire cost of food. Preschool education is the only education for which there is a charge. All other education in China is free.

Comrade Chiu explained somewhat apologetically that the equipment and level of education were "simple" and "low" because it is just a neighborhood kindergarten. Though three of the teachers have been trained as kindergarten teachers, some were housewives who had short periods of training, usually from three to six months, and the rest have simply had on-the-job training. All of the teachers live within the neighborhood.

The mothers of Fengsheng have alternative day-care options to sending their children to the local nursery. Many factories

have nursing rooms to which mothers can bring their babies
when their maternity leave is over. This is a most convenient
arrangement, as most Chinese women breast-feed their babies
and, in fact, may leave their work twice during the day to do so.
Many factories in which women work also have nurseries that
children may attend from approximately eighteen months until
three years. (Due to the decentralization of education and to
limited facilities, the ages at which children enter the various
stages of preschool care vary widely from city to city and even
from neighborhood to neighborhood within the same city. But,
of course, the greatest variation is between urban and rural preschool facilities.) Another option and one still favored by many
Chinese women is leaving their babies at home to be cared for
by the grandmother. Although reliable statistics do not exist at
this time, it was said that at least 50 percent of the children
under the age of three are cared for at home, usually by grandparents, only occasionally by the mothers themselves, and the
remainder are cared for in nursing rooms and nurseries. From
the age of three until the beginning of primary school at age
seven the number attending kindergarten rises to 80 percent in
the cities. The percentages for all age groups are far lower in
the countryside.

Sian

Most children attend nursery and kindergarten during the
day and return home every evening, but a few twenty-four-
hour kindergartens are in existence. One such "full-time"
kindergarten (twelve-hour-a-day kindergartens are known as
part-time!) is at Number 17 Ching Nian Lu in Sian. One hundred boys and girls live here from Monday morning until Saturday afternoon, when they return home to spend the weekend
with their parents. Li Chun, a small slightly built woman with
regular white teeth, short pigtails, and a large, round, serious
face which lights up quite suddenly when she smiles, is the

chairman of the revolutionary committee of the kindergarten. "Our main task," she stated quietly but clearly, "is to educate children from three to seven years. Our main focus is on language—telling stories, reading poems—but we also want to help the children to know society and nature. They sing songs and do dances, have physical exercises and active play. They study simple arithmetic to learn their numbers, and they paint, sometimes special subjects and other times whatever is in their minds.

"We also train the children to love the Communist party, to love Chairman Mao, and to love the socialist motherland," Comrade Li continued. "We stress politeness and sanitation and want them to have a good ideology. We want them to have good health and basic knowledge to prepare them for entering primary school."

The kindergarten is built, as are most of the buildings in Ching Nian Lu, around a series of courtyards. As Comrade Li and the other teachers move from class to class, speaking to a child here, giving another a passing hug, it is clear that they feel warm affection for the children and take obvious pleasure and pride in them.

Twenty-five five-year-olds sit in a semicircle, boys on one side, girls on the other, and accompanied by a teacher playing an organ, sing about a drum while pretending simultaneously to be playing one. They sing another song about playing a trumpet, acting it out all the while. And then, while they simultaneously chug-chug along, they sing that they are a train. They lift their arms as if to shoot while singing about shooting down an airplane and end with a rousing "Long live Chairman Mao."

Six-year-olds are sitting at individual desks, each with his own pile of crayons, drawing pictures with great concentration. They have been told that they should draw a picture of anything in their mind. One draws the sun, trees, and birds, another a boat, and another a snowman; many of the pictures are of tanks shooting. They are absorbed in their work and barely look up as the teachers or visitors look over their shoulders to watch. A large paper cutout of a soldier holding a gun is hanging on the wall.

After their classes the children stream out into the courtyard, and the teachers organize them into circle games in which the teachers participate with nearly as much enthusiasm as the children.

Shanghai

In the Kung Chiang New Village in Shanghai out of a total of 3,000 preschoolers, 2,200 children attend kindergarten. According to the teachers at a kindergarten that is associated with the Second Combined Primary School, children who remain at home with their family during their preschool years are "proud," whereas those who have been to kindergarten "have more knowledge, understand the teacher more easily, behave better, love labor, and obey discipline."

Four-year-olds pretending that they are carrying guns sing and dance that they are going on horseback to the Chinese-Russian border to see the People's Liberation Army. Three-and-a-half-year-olds are learning a poem. First the teacher says the entire poem; she then explains it one line at a time, and finally children repeat it line by line in unison:

> Listen, listen,
> Song of the airplane from the five continents,
> Foreign guests, foreign guests come to visit Peking.
> Welcome, welcome,
> The hearts of the people in the world connect
> Friendship between the people of the world
> Forever.

"Productive labor" is part of the regular responsibilities of five-and-a-half- and six-year-olds. They sit around small tables thirty minutes each week folding and stapling the boxes into which are packed the tiny light bulbs made by the housewives in the local neighborhood factory. They also help around the school by wiping the windows and cleaning the floors. Most schools do not employ cleaning help; it is felt that it is important for the children to do manual labor, to have some understanding of the life of workers and peasants, and to have concrete ways of contributing to their society.

In Shanghai's Second Combined Primary School all students begin to learn English, as they do throughout the city, in the fourth grade. Fifty-six sixth-graders sitting in four columns, fourteen students in each column from the front to the back of the room, are having an English lesson on the topic of China's National Day (October 1, the day the Communists took power in 1949). They are led by fourteen-year-old Liu Man-hung, her smile tentative but warm, her dark hair parted in the middle and falling into long pigtails down to the middle of her back, a striped blouse under her gray jacket and a red scarf around her neck signifying that she is a Little Red Guard. "Chairman Mao, Chairman Mao, you are the red sun in our hearts," shouts the class in unison with feeling. They recite the story of the revolution, which they have learned by heart in English, and they end by saying: "Now we all work very hard for the revolution, for world revolution. Today we all live a happy life, but we must remember class bitterness and class hatred. We must all remember Chairman Mao's teaching. Let's shout—'I love Tien An Men.'" At this point the entire class sings the popular children's song of the same name—in Chinese.

Their notebooks, written in clear round script, reflect the same emphasis on politics and on what is meaningful in their lives. In one notebook the following is written in perfect English:

October 1 is our National Day. The people in Shanghai warmly celebrate it. In the morning workers, peasants, soldiers

and Little Red Soldiers gather in the people's square. All of us
are very happy. We shout

"Long live the People's Republic of China!"
"Long live the Communist Party of China!"
"Long live our great leader Chairman Mao!"
"A long life to him!"

And in another notebook in equally perfect English and clear
handwriting:

Serve the people.
Granny Wang is over 60.
Her son is a P.L.A. man.
On Sunday we often go to her home.
We study Chairman Mao's work together with her.
We follow Chairman Mao's teaching
    Serve the People.
Clean the house, clean the windows
Some of us clean the tables and chairs.

We all work hard.

Back in Peking just down the street from the Ta Cheng
Kindergarten 805 students—435 boys and 370 girls—ranging
in age from seven to thirteen, attend the Chin Shih-feng Primary
School. According to Comrade Chang Yu-feng, the chairman of
the revolutionary committee, a young attractive woman wearing
a print blouse, her hair cut a little longer than the usual style,
"The children must have the social consciousness of the proletariat; they must learn for the revolution." Physical labor is
stressed in the primary school as one method of developing the
"social consciousness of the proletariat." The younger children
do two hours of physical labor every two weeks; the older ones
do one half hour a day. The students do farm work; they plant
trees, rake the grass, and spread fertilizer. They clean the play-
ground, carry coal, and have worked together with the teachers

to repair two buildings to be used for classrooms. And in the winter they clear away the snow.

Primary-school children in the Fengsheng school study mathematics, including the traditional Chinese method of counting using the abacus; they study Chinese language, including composition and the reading of newspapers, and politics, "social knowledge," painting, music, and physical exercise. Their day begins at 7:40 with the usual period of exercises; after listening to the radio for a brief time, they have four periods of classes. At 11:35 they leave school to return home for lunch and a rest, and at 2:00 school begins again. From then until 5:30 the students have two or three periods, and the Red Guards have their activities. At 5:30 they return home. The students have a four-week vacation in the summer and a four-week vacation in the winter, and the teachers have a two-week vacation each summer and winter.

Although grades were largely eliminated during the Cultural Revolution, Comrade Chang allowed that since the Cultural Revolution the children have tests and exams frequently during and at the end of the school term. Grades, or "points" as the Chinese say, are sent home twice a year. Comrade Chang insisted, however, that there is no competition even though there are grades and exams.

If the student is not doing well, the teacher contacts the parents, who then often come to school to discuss the problem. Possibly the teacher will help the child with his work, or other students might help him. In a discussion of whether children must repeat the same grade if they are not doing well the teachers allowed that before the Cultural Revolution students were kept back but since the Cultural Revolution educators are "still studying the issue." Comrade Chang clarified further, "Sometimes the child will repeat a grade if his points are very low, but we do not only consider his points, whether they are high or low; we consider the real level of the children. If a child can catch up, he will go on to the next grade even if he needs extra help. The classmates help each other after school hours and on holidays."

An active program of public-health education is directed toward the students in the primary school. Both through the teachers and through radio broadcasts attempts are made to teach the students the importance of sanitation. The students bring their own cups and handkerchiefs with them to school. They are expected to wash their hands before meals, and those students who are "on duty" check on cleanliness in the classroom. The school also provides immunizations for the children. Though they find that the children have very few illnesses, "they do sometimes catch colds."

If the student is only slightly ill, he will go home to rest; if he has a more severe illness, he will be taken by the parents to the neighborhood hospital. When the students get "influenza" in the winter, they use traditional Chinese medicines, and "the epidemic is usually controlled." But all infectious disease is reported to the Red Medical Worker in the lane health station. Sports are considered to be extremely important in conditioning the body to "combat illness"; in the winter particularly, the children are advised to do a lot of outdoor physical exercises and to run early in the morning. The teachers and staff members of the primary school obtain their medical care free from the Fengsheng Neighborhood Hospital; they have the usual fifty-six-day maternity leave and a physical examination once a year.

After school hours on a warm autumn Friday afternoon many of the children remaining in the school seem to be Red Guards or the younger version, Little Red Guards. Outside the front of the school a small group of Little Red Guards is practicing for a National Day performance, their red scarves tied loosely around their necks, singing and dancing about planting trees and sunflowers. A teacher in her early thirties wearing glasses, brown pants, and pigtails enthusiastically acts out the dance first; the children then imitate her and try it on their own. Elsewhere boys and girls, all Red Guards, practice their basketball, lining up to take turns shooting baskets. Thirteen-year-olds are meeting in a room in the top floor of the school and are discussing who should become a Red Guard. They sit around a long wooden table; a teacher is clearly in charge, and the students raise their hands from their elbows, which are firmly planted on the desk, before they speak. Everyone seems engrossed in the meeting.

"On behalf of the teachers, students, and Red Guards of this school, I want to welcome you to Middle School Number Thirty-one," Ma Wen-chen, the vice-chairman of the revolutionary committee, said warmly as he, several teachers, four students, and their guests sat around the conference table. Sixteen hundred students from the West District of Peking attend Middle School Number 31, continuing their education after completing five years of primary school. Comrade Ma described the history of the school: "The school was originally set up before Liberation by the British church. After Liberation when we took it over, middle school was popularized, and this school was enlarged. At the time of Liberation there were nine classes; now there are thirty-four.

"Since the Cultural Revolution we have shortened the course from six years to five years—three years for secondary middle school and two years for higher middle school. Middle schools are still experimenting with the number of years that are desirable. We now pay more attention to political education. Our country is a socialist country, and we must arm our students' minds with Marxism, Leninism, and Mao-Tse-tung Thought.

"Since the Cultural Revolution we have also tried to combine theory and practice. In the past, theory was separated from practice, but according to the May 7, 1966, directive, the students should learn about industry and agriculture as well as their academic subjects. Therefore, they now study in school for eight months, work in a factory for one month, work in the countryside for one month, and have two months vacation, one month in the summer and one in the winter. We want to train the students to have the habit of taking part in physical labor, to have the feelings of the workers and peasants, and to learn things they cannot learn in the classroom."

The school has four small workshops. In the first Chang Hsiao-hung, a thirteen-year-old first-year student who is also a Red Guard, described the production of amplifiers for the Second Electric Machine Factory in Peking. The shop was set up with the help of a female worker from a local factory who directs their work. When the students have mastered the techniques needed for producing the amplifiers, the worker will return to her factory. After the students have produced the amplifiers, they carefully check and pack them.

A fourteen-year-old English-speaking student, Shih Cheng-chang, described the work being done in the second shop, where students repair school-owned machinery under the dual direction of a math teacher and a retired worker who teaches the students the "good spirit of the workers." The third shop produces wire groups for trucks, and the fourth shop covers the wires, tests them, and sends them on to the factory. Wu Lan, a thirteen-year-old girl with a lively smile, commented, "Whenever we see a truck from the Peking branch number thirty bus company, we think of the contribution that we made toward producing that truck."

Middle School Number 31 is not under the jurisdiction of a neighborhood committee (its students come from many different neighborhoods) but rather is under the jurisdiction of Peking's West District. There are sixty middle schools in the West District, and though money is allocated by the district, the standards for these schools are set by the municipality. Thus the level of government responsible for the administration of the schools is often not the same as the level of government responsible for financing the schools. In Shanghai, for example, the Yang Pu district allocates money for the primary and middle schools within its boundaries, gives the money directly to the schools, and yet the schools within the Kung Chiang New Village are administered by the neighborhood committee. The committee is fully aware of the financial affairs of the schools, as there is an accountant at the neighborhood level who is "in charge of" the funds given to each school, and the proposed school budgets go through the committee.

Neighborhood administration of the schools has been part of the attempt to strengthen the role of the local neighborhoods since the Cultural Revolution, in effect an attempt to strengthen community control. But when the problem of how much community control is possible when a higher level controls the financing was raised, the vice-chairman of the revolutionary committee of the Kung Chiang New Village responded emphatically, "It is not the money that makes the decisions!" He went on to say, "What is important is the educational revolution in the schools, directing the ideological work of the teachers. If a teacher has problems with her political ideology, many people can help her to change her thinking, even the students. The teachers are responsible to the people, not to the government department which provides the money." Comrade Pan pointed out that it was community pressure and criticism that would effect change in the schools rather than the power of the purse.

It is, of course, extremely difficult to assess the real power of local Chinese neighborhoods as compared with the power of the district level and the power of the professional teachers, but it seems clear that local leaders are attempting to bolster that power. Interestingly, there was essentially no mention of parent participation except with regard to a specific child. The emphasis was rather on neighborhood control.

The middle school is administered by a revolutionary committee made up of eighteen members, of whom four are either members of the P.L.A. or of a workers' Mao Tse-tung propaganda team, six are administrative cadres, and the remaining eight are made up of three teachers, one worker in the school, and four students, some of whom are Red Guards.

Comrade Ma continued to describe the changes that had been made since the Cultural Revolution: "After Liberation all primary-school graduates could be admitted to middle schools, but they had to take an exam, and those that did better on the exam went to better schools. Since the Cultural Revolution the exam has been eliminated, and an attempt is being made to distribute students of varying abilities among all the schools. We were profoundly affected by the Cultural Revolution—at the beginning of nineteen sixty-six there were no courses given at all, and by the second half of nineteen sixty-six the entire school was closed. During this period the Red Guards traveled all over the country; some came to this school, and some went out into society to discuss and criticize the educational process. At the beginning of nineteen sixty-seven we gave a course in Mao Tse-tung Thought, and by the end of nineteen sixty-seven academic courses began again."

The classes are very large at the middle school—up to fifty students per class. The teachers would like to reduce the number of students in each class, but at this time that is not possible due to a shortage of both teachers and classrooms. Ninety teachers teach sixteen hundred students, and an additional sixty staff members work at the school. The teachers must have graduated from a university or from a high-level educational institute, and in addition, according to Comrade Ma, they must meet several requirements: They must be loyal to the party's educational policies; they must have the desire to train young people for the socialist motherland; they must study Marxism, Leninism, and Mao Tse-tung Thought; they must be very familiar with the courses that they teach; they must have good teaching methods; they must have some experience; and they must have good health. (The English teacher was particularly impressive at this middle school; he spoke impeccable American English and seemed to have warm rapport with the students.)

Ma Wen-chen also discussed the problem of grades. Middle School Number 31 currently uses grades that range from "excellent," which is five points, down to "failure," which is two points. They have two tests each term, one in the middle of the term and one at the end, but both teachers and students were extremely critical of excessive preoccupation with the number of points a student is getting. Currently grades are based not solely on academic achievement but also on ideology, the student's total state of knowledge, his attitude and purpose of study, and his physical training. Comrade Ma felt that in the past there was too much stress on exams and too much stress on grades. "Points were the lifeline of the student. The teachers used points to promote the students who studied hard, and they tried to make it hard for the students by giving them 'surprise attacks.' Now we use exams to promote study through review and to enable both the student and the teacher to understand the student's level of knowledge. Before the Cultural Revolution we only had closed-book exams; now we have both closed-book and open-book exams. Today we try not to put much stress on points but rather on social consciousness and cultural knowledge. We try to educate the students as to the purpose of their study and to teach them to serve the people and not themselves."

Wang Hsieh is a sixteen-year-old student in the first year of higher middle school. He takes eight subjects: politics, mathematics, English, Chinese, chemistry, physics, biology, and sports. Since he lives far from school, and since his parents both work, Wang Hsieh has his three meals in school, paying fourteen to fifteen yuan per month. About two hundred students out of the sixteen hundred eat all of their meals at school; an additional three hundred eat only lunch there. The students who eat their meals at school eat together with members of the faculty, who are also able to take their meals in the school cafeteria. Although the typical school day ends at four o'clock, most students stay in school until six for sports and "cultural activities."

Though Chinese schools offer some limited opportunities for fantasy or improvisation, oftentimes these opportunities yield highly politicized work, reflecting, at least in part, the highly politicized nature of the society. One example of such fantasy is a play written by seven students with the help of one of their teachers for a National Day observance. One student acted as the announcer and described the action while the others danced and acted out the story in pantomime. As the play opens, it is early morning, and fishermen are already out fishing in the South Sea in order to "serve socialist construction." They see a storm coming. As they "go to fight against the storm," they hear someone crying, "Help! Help!" After they rescue the drowning man, there is much dancing by the women's militia, the Red Guards, and the Little Red Guards who come to the shore to help and to see who has been rescued.

After the person is rescued, everyone in the town welcomes home the fishermen with their "bumper harvest of fish." The rescued man has escaped from Taiwan, where his father had been killed. Before going to meet his brother who has been living all the while on the mainland, he tells the townspeople that the people of Taiwan are suffering terribly; he dramatically describes his bitter life on Taiwan and states that the Taiwanese people are waiting for Liberation. The play ends with the announcer saying that the Taiwanese compatriots are class brothers and sisters and, finally, that "we must liberate Taiwan and wipe out the enemies. Under the leadership of Mao Tse-tung, we must advance forever."

CHAPTER 7

A WORLD IN WHICH WE CAN BE HUMAN

> ... how does it happen that everyone takes as zealous an interest in the affairs of his township, his county, and the whole state as if they were his own? It is because everyone, in his sphere, takes an active part in the government of society.
>
> —Alexis de Tocqueville,
> *Democracy in America*

> We seek a private house, a private means of transportation, a private garden, a private laundry.... We seek more and more privacy, and feel more and more alienated and lonely when we get it.
>
> —Philip Slater,
> *The Pursuit of Loneliness*

THE ORGANIZATION of life in China's neighborhoods can perhaps best be viewed as a total community support system, one fostered and maintained by the residents of the neighborhoods themselves. As life in the Fengsheng Neighborhood demonstrates, the people of China's cities have a myriad of ways in which they can interact: within their courtyard, where residents talk informally, communally clean the courtyard, plant and prune the greenery, admire one another's children, and discuss the latest political events; within their study group, where people read together, discuss politics, evaluate their own and others' attitudes and contributions, and are in turn evaluated; within the residents' committee, in which members are encouraged to help one another and to come together in large numbers for common purposes such as the Great Patriotic Sanitation Movement; within the neighborhood, where people work cooperatively to provide preschool care, to provide work for the unemployed in local factories, and to provide health care; and finally within the place of work, which provides not only study groups but a larger central focus, an avenue to contributing to the society, a parallel system of providing human services, and a setting for warm social relationships.

This total structure is characterized first by intimacy. People live and work together very closely and know each other well. The concept of privacy seems to be quite different in China, where an individual's personal life, his health, and his work performance are all viewed as being in the public domain, since they all affect the role he plays and the contribution he makes to society. The very structure of work and of residential communities, even the physical structure of the courtyards built within walls, serve to enhance this intimacy.

The second notable characteristic, one closely tied to the first and in fact made possible by such close relationships, is control. Just as one's personal affairs are a subject of concern for one's associates, so must one's antisocial ideas and deeds be a subject of concern. It was due to just such community concern and the exercise of community (even if "community" means the entire country) control that the Chinese have accomplished what is in the eyes of some Westerners an astonishing feat—the eradication of drug addiction and of venereal disease. But for a community to be able to exercise such control, the people must be willing to grant the necessary authority. The view, for example, that the individual has a right to choose a course of action that seems to harm only himself is not accepted in China. Whatever happens to each individual affects the entire society; there are no victimless crimes.

According to one observer of the Chinese legal system:

> Most people do not commit serious crimes without warning. Such actions are a part and perhaps the culmination of an entire pattern of dissatisfaction, unhappiness, or confusion. . . . The Chinese, through the small groups, treat these symptoms of unhappiness and possible deviation as soon as they appear. The effort is to solve problems before they get entirely out of control, somewhat like treating a physical disease.
>
> As a person begins to express improper thoughts or deviant tendencies, others will try to "help" him. This takes the form of criticizing the incorrect actions and explaining what would be correct. It also involves discovering and curing the root causes of the problem. For example, a person might be sloppy in his work and consequently damage production. He is criticized for his carelessness, but also he is given additional technical training to improve his skills. Moreover, other aspects of his life are examined to find the root causes of his difficulties. Perhaps an unhappy marriage is adversely affecting his work; if so, the factory group must find means of "helping" his family life.[1]

Thus the functioning of the entire person is seen as the concern of the community in which he lives and works, and that community is responsible for helping him, through criticism, support, and if necessary, through modifying his environment. This amount of peer or societal control would, no doubt, be intolerable to many in the West, but it seems to be accepted, by and large, by the Chinese, and indeed it seems to stem at least in part from their past. The individual's right to self-determination, to personal growth, or even to self-destruction has never been revered in China as it is in the West.

A third characteristic of life in China's neighborhoods and places of work is the number of warm relationships an individual is likely to have. In addition to the marital relationship and the parent-child relationship, an adult may well have a warm relationship with his/her parents, neighbors, friends, and co-workers. This phenomenon is at least a partial explanation of the seeming acceptance on the part of married couples of their living and working in different cities. One is not so completely dependent on one's spouse; there are others with whom one interacts with warmth and mutual dependence.

In conjunction with the multiplicity of warm relationships, people have the opportunity to play a variety of roles at every stage of life. With one's child one can be nurturing; with one's parents one can be nurtured. A member of a residents' committee can at one time help a neighbor; at another time she may herself be the one who is helped. In the factory a group leader can be both the one who is criticized and the critic; a shop foreman can be teacher and student. A student may at one moment be the pupil and the next moment be teaching another student. An elderly person can both help his neighbors and be helped by others. One characteristic does not rigidly define the individual. A person who has a chronic illness and needs constant help may be a group leader; the young teach the old as in the "Each One Teach One" efforts of the 1950's; the intellectuals go to the countryside to learn from the poor and often illiterate peasants. People are not artificially locked into their roles in the way so many people in our society are because of both the limited variety of relationships and the limits that class and status place on the individual.

Philip Slater in his book *The Pursuit of Loneliness* discusses the ways in which we in our society suppress conflicting needs and emotions:

> These opposing forces are much more equally balanced than the society's participants like to recognize—were this not true

there would be no need for suppression. Life would indeed be much less frantic if we were all able to recognize the diversity of responses and feelings within ourselves, and could abandon our somewhat futile efforts to present a monolithic self-portrait to the world.[2]

How much differently might poor mothers on welfare feel about themselves and how much richer our society would be if they were to teach in the schools about the "bitter past" and the still bitter present. There have been recent efforts to utilize the elderly as foster grandparents or in work with the retarded[3] and to establish programs in which "kids teach kids,"[4] but these efforts are negligible compared to the need—on the part of helper as well as those who need to be helped. We clearly need to be able to act out many different roles and feelings; the helper must sometimes be the helped; the therapist, the patient; the teacher, the student.

In part what makes it possible for people in China to play various roles within their communities is a strong element of deprofessionalization. Human services are provided at the lowest level of organization largely by nonprofessionals recruited from the communities in which they live. Local health workers are trained for brief periods of time in the hope of eliminating the alienation that occurs during extended educational experiences and in the hope of decreasing the distance between the helper and the helped. Most social services are provided by residents with no training but with a knack for dealing with others' problems. Marital disputes, interfamilial disputes, welfare problems, and problems of the aged are all handled by indigenous leaders in the residents' committees and in the neighborhoods or in the places of work. The elderly themselves are used extensively in these roles, thereby drawing on their traditional respected role within the community, their experience and talent, their ability to compare the "bitter past" to the present, and another great asset, their free time. The Chinese do not want to waste any talent; it is one of their greatest strengths that a meaningful way to contribute is found for people at all ages and levels of accomplishment—from the five-year-olds folding boxes in the kindergarten to the elderly group leaders helping their neighbors to solve their differences. This feeling of being needed, of fulfilling a function beyond the scope of one's own needs, gives people both a sense of self-worth and a sense of connection with the wider environment. Furthermore, structuring a society in which most people have a meaningful function reduces the sense of alienation that so characterizes our era.

Connected with the utilization of talent at all levels and with the deprofessionalization, whenever possible, of health and welfare services is the companion result—demystification. If primary health care at the local level can be provided by Red Medical Workers who were formerly housewives and who have had only three to six months of training, then what can be so mystical, so special, so technical and difficult to grasp, about medical care? If people are urged at every level to participate in community health and in their own health care—even patients in psychiatric hospitals are told their diagnoses and exhorted to work with the psychiatric personnel to understand the causes of the disease—then medicine can no longer be viewed as a magical art/science with rituals that can be performed only by specially anointed priests. Mao urges everyone to participate, to taste the pear, and in that way to understand the pear. If one's elderly untrained neighbor down the street, a friend whom one has known for years, who speaks the same language, belongs to the same economic class, holds similar values, and lives in the same life-style, does marital counseling in the residents' committee, how mysterious and unfathomable could marital counseling be?

Concomitant with demystification is the peculiarly Chinese emphasis on self-reliance, a self-reliance that is collective in nature. A job, food, a roof, and basic medical care are guaranteed, but in addition the individual citizen within his local collective is encouraged to initiate ideas, to innovate, to work together with others to improve his environment. Thus a neighborhood factory must exist on its meager income at first, its employees earning a minimal salary, until step by step the income increases and subsequently salaries increase. The nursery-kindergarten begins with a few children and fewer teachers, supported only by parental fees and by the local neighborhood, and it gradually develops into a larger, smoothly functioning institution. The emphasis is on decentralization, on encouraging those at the local level to build their facilities themselves with minimal support from the city, the province, or the central government. Clearly the focus on self-reliance and local autonomy has been developed and fostered in large measure because of economic conditions, but it has also been fostered for political reasons. Neighborhood residents encouraged to develop their own satellite factories and local health stations, and peasants in the countryside urged to follow the example of the famous Tachai Production Brigade and develop their communes through "hard work" and "self-reliance," must, in order to work effectively, be aware of the political and economic goals of the society, must be knowledgeable about local political and economic conditions, must be able to work within a group to determine priorities and methods, and, in sum, must be active participants in the society. And that, clearly, is the Chinese goal—to encourage as many of the nearly 800,000,000 Chinese as possible to become active participants.

One of the central problems or contradictions of this approach is that special-interest groups and their goals sometimes get short shrift. The process of women's liberation is an excellent example of conflicting goals within China's development. The role of women in China has undergone a revolutionary transformation since 1949. The central government has taken active steps to guarantee women basic human rights. The 1950 Marriage Law abolished arranged marriages, outlawed paying any price in money or goods for a wife, outlawed polygamy, concubines, and child marriage, and guaranteed the right of divorce to the wife as well as to the husband. The central government has also had a strong equal-pay-for-equal-work policy.

However, the continuation and extension of that liberation has been slowed by many factors: the continued existence of "feudal ideology" on the part of women themselves, men, and the elderly, who still have substantial influence; the lack of sufficient jobs for all women in the rural as well as the urban areas; and the economic and political policy of encouraging decentralization and self-reliance. A commune, for example, in addition to a basic concern about the rights of women, must also be concerned with maximizing crop production, developing small industries, providing educational and health services, developing political leadership, and a host of other issues. The liberation of women must be seen in this total context as one imperative among many, as a thread that runs through all of the areas of concern and development. Inevitably there have been visitors from the United States who have criticized the progress made by China's women. And yes, many of China's women do not have full-time, year-round work, particularly in the countryside; and yes, many of China's women still suffer inequities in the rural "work point" system of determining wages; and yes, many traditional female professions such as nursery and kindergarten teaching have not been opened to men; and yes, there are not sufficient preschool facilities to meet the needs of working women; and yes, there are relatively few women in leadership positions. The Chinese recognize many of these remaining inequities. Moreover, they feel that there is much in Chinese life that needs to be improved for both men and women—the long hours that peasants must work on the communes, inadequate health care in the more remote areas, insufficient technological development countrywide, a shortage of both teachers and classrooms, a persisting discrepancy between the standard of living in the cities and the standard of living in the countryside, and a host of other severe problems that must be dealt with continuously. And one of these, and only one, is the liberation of women. Perhaps Linda Gordon, in her perceptive article "The Fourth Mountain: Women in China," sums it up most succinctly: "In China the process of women's liberation cannot be understood separately from the process of the entire revolution."[5] Furthermore, the liberation of women is seen by Chinese women themselves as "being able to work and contribute in the building of the new China."[6]

This feeling of commitment, of working for a cause greater than oneself, has been described by many China observers. Recent visitors to China have returned to the West describing a country with a "high pitch of collective spirit,"[7] a "sense of purpose, self-confidence, and dignity,"[8] and a "deep sense of mission."[9] The Chinese refer to this spirit as "revolutionary optimism," a concept that "the Chinese people are part of the revolution, a revolution which will ultimately be victorious. No matter what the difficulties, the individual will have a bright future."[10] The physically or emotionally ill patient is urged to obtain treatment and to overcome his problems not only for his own sake but also for the sake of the revolution. A couple involved in a marital dispute is urged to "unite" for the sake of the revolution. Students are exhorted to study for the revolution. The individual is urged to subordinate his own feelings to the larger cause. As one observer has written of the Chinese revolutionary view of the new man: "Losing his own individual identity, he partakes of the greater spirit of the group and thereby achieves a spiritual transformation."[11]

Taking part in the greater spirit of the group, the belief in goals beyond one's own personal happiness and well-being and even beyond the happiness and well-being of one's family, can make many difficult, hard-to-bear aspects of life not only tolerable but possibly even meaningful. Many Chinese workers and peasants, of course, do highly repetitive work, and educated men and women spend a certain proportion of their time doing manual labor, but such work takes on an added dimension, a new and very different meaning, if it is viewed as part of a cooperative striving to reach a greater goal, a goal one fervently believes in.

The contrast is striking between the sense of commitment, of cooperation, of relatedness, evident in China's neighborhoods and the picture of American society vividly described by Philip Slater. He claims that "Americans have voluntarily created and voluntarily maintained a society which increasingly frustrates and aggravates" three basic human desires—"the desire for *community*," "the desire for *engagement*," and "the desire for *dependence*."[12] The question that must be raised is, What is the relevance of the organization of China's cities to us in the West? What is the relevance of Red Medical Workers, neighborhood hospitals, residents' committees with locally selected leadership, small satellite factories, study groups, and small children singing about Chairman Mao? What can we learn from a culture whose cities have lent a sense of community for centuries by virtue of the traditional architecture and city planning? What can we learn from the urban organization of a society whose revolutionary values stress collectivity and cooperation rather than individualism and competition? What can our postindustrial, media-barraged communities, whose residents often relate more intensively to television programs and personalities than to life around them, learn from the technologically underdeveloped Chinese society in which neighborhood life and daily work are still intensely meaningful?

Although technology has simplified our lives enormously, it is also a primary cause of our isolation. We may be a long way

from washing our clothes in a stream, as do some Chinese
women, simultaneously exchanging news and personal advice
with the other women of the village, but we are also moving
away from the local laundromat or the apartment laundry room
where one can get a sense of those who live nearby. Not only
do our washers and dryers make it possible to do our laundry
in isolation, but our telephones and televisions, while on the one
hand putting us in touch with others, on the other hand separate
us by keeping us within our homes. Even our kitchen appliances
encourage less and less communication within the family.
(Ralph Keyes, in his aptly titled book *We, the Lonely People:
Searching for Community*, quotes a mother talking about the
generation gap: "I'm gonna tell you what brought on the whole
thing—dishwashers. That's right, dishwashers. I got to know
my kids better, they told me more, when we washed dishes together. One would wash, another rinse, and a third dry. We'd
fight but we'd also talk. Now that we have a dishwasher, there's
no regular time when we get to know each other."[13])

The hope, of course, was that with more technology, with
more conveniences, we would be freed from physical labor and
have more time to "communicate," to "relate meaningfully to
one another." But we are learning that perhaps communication
takes place around shared activity, mundane, everyday activity
such as commuting to work together, making dinner, or doing
the dishes. It is extremely difficult for people to talk about what
is on their minds without a warm-up period, without structure
around which to talk, without shared experiences. And yet we
seek greater and greater privacy, privacy that will inevitably
diminish the number and depth of our human relationships.

We seek a private house, a private means of transportation, a
private garden, a private laundry, self-service stores, and do-it-
yourself skills of every kind. An enormous technology seems to
have set itself the task of making it unnecessary for one human

being ever to ask anything of another in the course of going about his daily business. Even within the family Americans are unique in their feeling that each member should have a separate room, and even a separate telephone, television, and car, when economically possible. We seek more and more privacy, and feel more and more alienated and lonely when we get it.[14]

What can we learn from the Chinese as we try to build bridges to one another, to form a new sense of community? We can learn that we need not rely solely on professionals in order to care for one another, that ordinary untrained people can reach out if permitted and encouraged to do so, and that they can help to provide health care, emotional support, physical attention, and above all the feeling that someone cares. We can learn that giving is as important, perhaps, as any other human need and that by providing mechanisms for people to give to one another we humanize all of us.

In his study of blood donors in several societies, Richard M. Titmuss describes the motivations of the voluntary blood donors he interviewed:

> They acknowledged that they could not and should not live entirely as they may have liked if they had paid regard solely to their own immediate gratifications. To the philosopher's question "what kind of actions ought we to perform?" they replied, in effect, "those which will cause more good to exist in the universe than there would otherwise be if we did not so act."[15]

In further discussing the right to give and the limitation on the individual's freedom if he is denied that right, Titmuss continues:

> In a positive sense we believe that policy and processes should enable men to be free to choose to give to unnamed strangers.

> ... If it is accepted that man has a social and a biological need to help, then to deny him opportunities to express this need is to deny him the freedom to enter into gift relationships.[16]

We must learn that people need to be involved in their own care, that technology alone will not necessarily raise health indices or reading levels but that health care, education, solving problems such as drug abuse, alcoholism, or the spiraling rate of venereal disease must be tied to massive social, political, and economic changes within the society and must be meaningful, must make sense, to the population for massive change to occur. Nowhere is this better illustrated perhaps than in the area of population control. Massive efforts have been made all over the world to lower population growth, and these efforts have often met with failure.[17] But there have been astonishing successes in some of China's cities.[18] These have been due to, I believe, (1) the politicization of the issue of birth control (i.e., limiting the number of children one has is a *political* act done to help China and done in a context in which such political acts are expected and rewarded); (2) an intensive educational campaign conducted door-to-door by indigenous medical workers who are friends and neighbors of the women involved; and (3) a strong belief in "mass participation" in which one's use of "planned birth" is seen as participating in society and ultimately is seen as enabling women, particularly, to make an even greater contribution to China, to more effectively "hold up half of heaven," as Mao is quoted as saying. The provision of contraceptives alone would not have made the difference; even the recruitment of paraprofessionals to do community education would not have been enough. The birth-control effort in China must be seen as part of a much larger effort to involve the people in their own destiny.

Margaret Mead has stated that "the continuity of all cultures depends on the living presence of at least three generations."[19]

And elsewhere she has elaborated on this theme: "In the presence of grandparent and grandchild, past and future merge in the present. . . . For seeing a child as one's grandchild, one can visualize that same child as a grandparent, and with the eyes of another generation one can see other children . . . who must be taken into account—now. . . . the human unit of time . . . [is] the space between a grandfather's memory of his own childhood and a grandson's knowledge of those memories as he heard about them. We speak a great deal about a human scale; we need also a human unit in which to think about time."[20]

This, too, we can learn from the Chinese—that in order to maintain a continuity, a connectedness within society, the ties between the generations must be preserved, that even in the massive effort of the Chinese to "root out feudal ideology," they have not severed the bonds between grandparent, parent, and grandchild, but rather they have strengthened them. The physician with whom we traveled in 1972 described the Chinese family structure as one in which "the old take care of the young and the middle-aged take care of the old." Thus, the three-generational family is seen as a mini-collective, a small mutual-aid group. And when there are differences, as there are, when the elderly hold firm to their "old ideas" and try to convince the young, they are not shunted away and ignored. In the Chinese idiom these ideas are "struggled with"; they are discussed and debated until some solution can be agreed upon. In this way conflict is not avoided but rather dealt with directly.

Perhaps we can also learn from the Chinese that there must be a meaning to life outside of personal happiness and personal fulfillment, that human beings thrive on a commitment to a cause greater than themselves, their family, and their immediate group. Perhaps this can be seen most clearly by looking at China's children, who seem to feel that there is a place in society for them, that there are ways for them to contribute, that they are needed. Perhaps what plagues so many of the young and the old, the poor, the sick, and the unemployed in our own society is the feeling of being extraneous, of not being necessary to the workings of society and often of not being wanted.

We clearly cannot superimpose Chinese solutions onto our problems; we must look to our own heritage, traditions, and culture for possible answers. Alexis de Tocqueville, who closely examined life in the United States in the second quarter of the nineteenth century, observed how actively Americans of that era participated in their society:

> How does it happen that in the United States, where the inhabitants have only recently immigrated to the land which they now occupy, and brought neither customs nor traditions with them there; where they met one another for the first time with no previous acquaintance; where, in short, the instinctive love of country can scarcely exist; how does it happen that everyone takes as zealous an interest in the affairs of his township, his county, and the whole state as if they were his own? It is because everyone, in his sphere, takes an active part in the government of society.[21]

De Tocqueville himself in his description of life in the New England townships answered his own question. Americans participated actively in their society because it was in their self-interest to do so:

> The native of New England is attached to his township because it is independent and free: his co-operation in its affairs ensures his attachment to its interests; the well-being it affords him secures his affection; and its welfare is the aim of his ambition and of his future exertions. He takes a part in every occurrence in the place; he practices the art of government in the small sphere within his reach.[22]

Perhaps once again it is in our self-interest to "take part in every occurrence," to "practice the art of government," to maximize opportunities for caring for one another, for working with one another. It is to be hoped that a deeper understanding of the ways in which our neighbors the Chinese are attempting to solve their problems can help us in the difficult and painful but not insurmountable task of solving our own. We must strive toward a more humane society, one that, in the words of Felix Greene, "doesn't divide us from one another, . . . releases us from the prison, the small boring world of me, [one] which allows us to be members of a community . . . [part of] a world in which we can be really human."[23]

NOTES

[1] Victor H. Li, "Law and Penology: Systems of Reform and Correction," in Michel Oksenberg, ed., *China's Developmental Experience*, New York, Columbia University, *Proceedings of the Academy of Political Science*, Vol. XXXI, No. 1 (March, 1973), pp. 152–153.

[2] Philip Slater, *The Pursuit of Loneliness* (Boston: Beacon Press, 1970), p. 4.

[3] "The Retarded and the Volunteer Helpers—They Need Each Other," *The New York Times*, November 27, 1971, p. 36.

[4] Alan Gartner, Mary Kohler, and Frank Riessman, *Children Teach Children: Learning by Teaching* (New York: Harper and Row, 1971).

[5] Linda Gordon, "The Fourth Mountain: Women in China," *Working Papers for a New Society*, Vol. I, No. 3 (Fall, 1973), pp. 27–39.

[6] Committee of Concerned Asian Scholars, *China! Inside the People's Republic* (New York: Bantam Books, 1972), p. 292.

[7] Ross Terrill, *800,000,000: The Real China* (Boston: Little Brown and Company, 1972), p. 227.

[8] Barbara W. Tuchman, *Notes from China* (New York: Collier Books, 1972), p. 3.

[9] Ruth and Victor Sidel, "The Human Services in China," *Social Policy*, Vol. II, No. 6, pp. 25–34.

[10] My appreciation to Dr. Wu Chen-i, professor of psychiatry, Peking Medical College, and Dr. Shen Yu-chun, director of the Department of Psychiatry, Peking Medical College, for elucidating the concept of "revolutionary optimism."

[11] Michel Oksenberg, *China: The Convulsive Society*, Headline Series, The Foreign Policy Association, No. 203 (December, 1970), p. 8.

[12] Slater, p. 5.

[13] Ralph Keyes, *We, the Lonely People: Searching for Community* (New York: Harper and Row, 1973), p. 33.

[14] Slater, p. 7.

[15] Richard M. Titmuss, *The Gift Relationship: From Human Blood to Social Policy* (New York: Pantheon Books, 1971), pp. 237–238.

[16] *Ibid.*, pp. 242–243.

[17] For further elucidation of this issue, see Aaron Segal, "The Rich, the Poor and Population," *Demography India*, Vol. II, No. 1 (1973), pp. 5–17, and J. Mayone Stycos, "Birth Control Clinics in Crowded Puerto Rico," in Benjamin D. Paul, ed., *Health, Culture, and Community* (New York: Russell Sage Foundation, 1955), pp. 189–210.

[18] Steven H. Lamm and Victor W. Sidel, "Analysis of Preliminary Public Health Data for Shanghai, 1972, Appendix E," in Victor W. Sidel and Ruth Sidel, *Serve the People: Observations on Medicine in the People's Republic of China* (New York: Josiah Macy, Jr. Foundation, 1973), pp. 243–255.

[19] Margaret Mead, *Culture and Commitment: A Study of the Generation Gap* (New York: Natural History Press/Doubleday and Company, Inc., 1970), p. 2.

[20] Margaret Mead, *Blackberry Winter: My Earlier Years* (New York: Simon and Schuster, 1972), pp. 282–284.

[21] Alexis de Tocqueville, *Democracy in America* (New York: Vintage Books, 1954), pp. 252–253.

[22] *Ibid.*, p. 71.

[23] Felix Greene, "Free to Be Human," *Far East Reporter: The New Human Being in the People's Republic of China*, April, 1973, pp. 4–11.

BIBLIOGRAPHY

Chang Sen-dou. "The Historical Trend of Chinese Urbanization," *Annals of the Association of American Geographers*, Vol. LIII, No. 2 (June, 1963), pp. 109–143.

Chen Pi-chao. "Overurbanization, Rustification of Urban-Educated Youths, and Politics of Rural Transformation," *Comparative Politics*, April, 1972, pp. 361–386.

Committee of Concerned Asian Scholars. *China! Inside the People's Republic*. New York: Bantam Books, 1972.

Gurley, John G. "Capitalist and Maoist Economic Development," in Edward Friedman and Mark Selden, eds., *America's Asia: Dissenting Essays on Asian-American Relations*. New York: Vintage Books, 1971.

Han Suyin. "Reflections on Social Change," *Bulletin of the Atomic Scientists*, Vol. XXII, No. 6 (June, 1966), pp. 80–83.

Hinton, William. *Hundred Day War: The Cultural Revolution at Tsinghua University*. New York: Monthly Review Press, 1972.

Lewis, John Wilson, ed. *The City in Communist China*. Stanford, Calif.: Stanford University Press, 1971.

Needham, Joseph. *The Grand Titration: Science and Society in East and West*. London: George Allen & Unwin, Ltd., 1969.

Oksenberg, Michel, ed. *China's Developmental Experience*. New York, Columbia University, *Proceedings of the Academy of Political Science*, Vol. XXXI, No. 1 (March, 1973).

"Our Neighborhood," *China Reconstructs*, Vol. XXII, No. 8 (August, 1973), pp. 2–11.

Robinson, Joan. *The Cultural Revolution in China*. Baltimore, Md.: Penguin Books, 1969.

Salaff, Janet Weitzner. "The Urban Communes and Anti-City Experience in Communist China," *China Quarterly*, Vol. XXIX (January, 1967), pp. 82–109.

Schurmann, Franz. *Ideology and Organization in Communist China*. Berkeley, Calif.: University of California Press, 1966.

Sidel, Ruth. "The Role of Revolutionary Optimism in the Treatment of Mental Illness in the People's Republic of China," *American Journal of Orthopsychiatry*, Vol. XLIII, No. 5 (October, 1973), pp. 732–736.

————. "Social Services in China," *Social Work*, Vol. XVII, No. 6 (November, 1972), pp. 5–13.

Sidel, Victor W., and Sidel, Ruth. *Serve the People: Observations on Medicine in the People's Republic of China.* New York: Josiah Macy, Jr. Foundation, 1973.

Snow, Edgar. *Red China Today.* New York: Vintage Books, 1971.

Terrill, Ross. *800,000,000: The Real China.* Boston: Little, Brown and Company, 1972.

Trewartha, Glenn T. "Chinese Cities: Origins and Functions," *Annals of the Association of American Geographers*, Vol. XLII, No. 1 (March, 1952), pp. 69–93.

Vogel, Ezra. *Canton under Communism.* New York: Harper and Row, 1969.

CHINA BOOKS & CRAFTS
101 CHERRY STREET
SEATTLE, WASHINGTON 98104